LIFE HAPPENS

A Memoir

LIFE HAPPENS

A Memoir

by

E. D. Clapham

DIADEM BOOKS

LIFE HAPPENS: A Memoir
All Rights Reserved. Copyright © 2015 E. D. Clapham

No part of this book may be reproduced or transmitted in any form or by any means, graphic, electronic, or mechanical, including photocopying, recording, taping or by any information storage or retrieval system, without the permission in writing from the copyright holder.

The right of Eleanor Clapham to be identified as the author of this work has been asserted in accordance with the Copyright, Designs and Patents Act 1988 sections 77 and 78.

Some names and identifying details have been changed to protect the privacy of individuals.

Front cover shows Author with 'Jo', about 1937

Published by Diadem Books
For information, please contact:
Diadem Books
16 Lethen View
Tullibody
ALLOA
FK10 2GE
Scotland UK

www.diadembooks.com

The views expressed in this work are solely those of the author and do not necessarily reflect the views of the publisher, and the publisher hereby disclaims any responsibility for them.

ISBN: 978-1-326-35277-6

For Leonard and Vee

Acknowledgements

Sincere and grateful thanks are due to:

Whitby U3A Creative Writing Group
Bernard Nelson of Whitby
Amanda Cowens of Whitby
My Family

For their Inspiration, Help, Time, Encouragement,
Love, Friendship and just for being who they are.

Prologue

NO-ONE IS RESPONSIBLE for how, where, or to whom they are born are they? That comes later, being responsible I mean, when we realise if we're lucky, that we have choices.

Of course luck has a lot to do with it and I should know, having had more than my fair share of it; but in spite of the luck I didn't fully accept that I had choices for a long, long time.

Also, some time ago, I made a decision to stop using the word 'should' and replace it with 'it would be', or 'have been, better if…' I just stopped 'shoulding' myself and others.

Okay, before you tell me I've used 'should' already in the first paragraph I need to say that decisions aren't laws, so as I fondly believe I am a fully paid up member of the human race, (i.e. 'imperfect'), I slip up now and again. If this bit of hard won philosophy has always been obvious to you then you are wiser or luckier than I have been. I've had to make a lot of mistakes and own them too before I could say 'it would have been better if…' Of course I accept that other people can and will continue to use the word 'should' to their heart's content, and so be it.

So back to being born and the situation each one of us has to accept and cope with whether good or bad. My situation and imperfect life that followed is the only one I can tell you about in complete honesty, so that's what I am going to do. I hope you stay with me on the first part of my journey, and meet the people who shared parts of it with me and the lessons I've learned from my mistakes and choices

Chapter One

To Begin With

I JOINED THE WORLD almost mid-way between the First and Second World Wars, being born at a house called 'Whitehaven' on the corner of Upgang Lane and Crescent Avenue in the small town of Whitby on the wild North East coast of Yorkshire, England. It was also, although obviously I wasn't aware of it then, during a huge economic crisis The Big Depression. I like to think my arrival cheered my folks up a bit: I expect the Doc (or the midwife) said 'It's a girl!' and they'd be pleased because they already had a boy, my brother Peter, four years before me, and that was it, no more children came along; so that was my immediate family – four of us; well, five actually, because at the time we lived with my Daddy's Mother, my Granma Nell, but I never really knew her because she died soon after I arrived. She can't have been very old but people often did die young then, before Penicillin and all the rest of it.

My Grandfather, Nell's husband, had died some years before in York where they lived before moving to Whitby. Uncle Ernest, my Daddy's older brother, had been killed in the war, which was supposed to be the war to end all wars, but of course it wasn't, was it? Being minus one, of course, I had no idea that the country and those around me were struggling to recover from the awful effects of one war whilst out of their sight across the English Channel a crazy little German corporal called Adolph Hitler was planning to take over the world in what would be World War 2.

Most families had lost at least one close relative or friend in the 1914–18 war, or during the widespread 'flu epidemic just after it. And there must have been plenty to be depressed about along with the economy; but naturally at this point I knew nothing about any of that, especially, as I was soon to learn, no-one spoke about losses, or feelings or the past, it just wasn't done. Good feelings were okay within reason and expressed calmly, but bad feelings were really out of bounds, hushed up or dismissed with a sharp 'cheer up' or, even worse, 'pull yourself together'. I've never found out how to do that, have you? pull myself together, I mean! Where would you start? No idea. Well eventually after a long time sort of muddling through life and not managing to 'pull myself together' I did discover how to be honest about my feelings and how to be responsible for and handle them, and I didn't learn that in any formal education or even from my parents.

Not long after my arrival Whitehaven was sold and we moved to a four-story Edwardian terrace house in Church Square only a few hundred yards away and closer to the cliff side, the Promenade and the ocean. Actually Church Square isn't a complete square; the top part was left open to fields known as Tucker's Fields and the largest church in town, St Hildas, sits in the centre of it, hence the name. There are quite a few unfinished parts of the town, ambitious projects which probably ran out of money but I think they just add to its uniqueness.

The surrounding area of the County used to be known as the North Riding, but at some point those 'powers that be' decided to do away with that interesting part of our heritage, along with the other two Ridings, East and West, for no apparent reason that I can think of except that politicians seem to do these things every now and then usually for some political gain or other. But enough of that for now, and anyway

Yorkshire folk still refer to 'The Ridings' and believe their county to be God's Own.

Being at the top of the west cliff was more or less the best place to be. It was the newer part. The east cliff was the original old town, historical, and quaint with alleyways called yards, some with steps leading down to the harbour where the fishing and sailing folk lived in their little huddled together, centuries-old homes and in other houses which were built into the cliff face below the church and the ancient ruined Abbey both of which still perch precariously on the cliff top. This part of town dates back hundreds of years and has a rich history. The narrow streets are still paved with the same original cobblestones and the many remaining cottages and little shops, with their bowed windows are reminiscent of a Dickens tale.

The river runs between the two cliffs and when in the 17th century the harbour became one of the country's busiest ports, and shipbuilding was also developed, so the west side also grew. Trading opened up, shops and homes were built along the quay, and then further up and atop the west cliff. Of course it became necessary to have a bridge to link the old and newer parts of the town and originally that was a drawbridge type which allowed the tall sailing ships through to their berths in the upper harbour and again when they sailed out and away, as did Captain James Cook when he set off from Whitby, where he had studied Navigation, to discover lands on the other side of the world which we now know as Australia and New Zealand.

I imagine that before the bridge, communication between the east and west folk was limited. Building the bridge changed that and the town became more united, and like all small towns it had and still has its fair share of drama, jealousies, eccentrics, intrigue and gossip; but natives of the town and those who choose to live there think it's unique and very special. A local saying is, 'There's the right way, the wrong way and then there's the Whitby way!'

As the 20th century dawned and motorised transport began to rival the horse-drawn kind across the old bridge, an updated swing bridge, wider and stronger, was constructed and welcomed by the growing number of townsfolk. However, it still had to swing open to allow the tall ships and other craft through, requiring pedestrians to wait patiently at both ends, as they still do.

Anyway, back to me and my family. I've told you about the close ones at No 4 Church Square, my future Daddy and Grandma, who had moved to the town after my Grandfather passed away. I think he had been a farmer and owned quite a lot of land near York. I don't know anything about that side of things, as I've already said, no-one ever talked about past things like that. I don't think they were hiding anything and there wasn't any whispering or mystery, it just never came up and I didn't ask. I don't ever remember being encouraged to be inquisitive, quite the opposite really; 'seen and not heard' was the order of the day for young people in those days, y'know! So as you can imagine, it did actually take me many years to speak up for myself, and others, about more or less anything, and also of course to stop 'shoulding'. I don't blame my parents or anyone else for that, it's just the way it was. Times were changing rapidly, younger people were anxious to 'keep up' and to 'be modern' yet at the same time were mindful of the accepted values of the time, discipline, respect and courtesy and a certain way of doing things.

About my Mother's side of the family, well, they were rooted in the town, mostly born, lived and died there probably without ever leaving, like most folk at that time, I imagine. Don't forget, rail travel was still quite an adventure, automobiles were few and far between, and as I've already said, the town was surrounded by moorland. Boys grew up believing their future was either Fishing or joining the Merchant Navy; girls thought theirs was to marry them, mend nets, gut fish and pray the men got back safely. However, the Great War (1914–1918) had brought about changes. The rigid class system had been shaken and stirred as people from all levels of society fought and worked side by side, causing new connections and friendships and the beginning of what became a much less formal way of life and a narrowing of the gap between rich and poor. Women had taken over men's work while they were away in the war and felt good about it and consequently better about themselves.

The decade known as the Roaring Twenties followed those war years and brought about a more light-hearted way of socialising and then of course there arrived the magic of the Movies which were called the Pictures, or the Flicks after the flickering of those early films and which further broadened people's minds, ideas and dreams and eventually, were to make a big impression on me and my dreams. I had entered what was to be both a difficult but also an exciting and changing era.

In 1918 she who would become my 'Mums' was aged 16. Her name was Vera but she was always called Vee. Three years earlier when only 13, her mother had died of Cancer and they had also not long before that lost her baby sister Norah aged only 5 from Pneumonia. Her only other sibling, an older brother Alan, had married and departed to live and work in London so people were starting to move around and widen their horizons; but this left Vee and her father grieving and alone so he decided to sell their house called Ledbury, (strange name!) in Crescent Avenue and move back to live with his elderly parents and two as yet unmarried sisters, Sally and Nan, still living at the original family home slightly down the hill towards the town centre and known as Havelock Place. Another sister, Esther, had married a soldier from New Zealand and gone there to live, a huge decision and adventure then, even more so than now, but a happier outcome from that dreadful time even though we never saw her again.

There were two other brothers in the family, uncles to Vee. They were called John and Arthur. They were both married and living and working in the town although they didn't seem to feature much in her life, or in mine come to think of it. I do remember John as a large, burly man who always had a pipe in his mouth and Arthur was the complete opposite, small, neat and jolly. John married a Catholic lady called Hannah and they had two sons and two daughters. Arthur and his equally jolly wife, Cecily (called Sissy), had three daughters who were all a lot older than me. I just knew they were there and where they lived and would see them occasionally around town. Their names were Dorothy, Lorna and Leila and I remember Mums once telling me that she had suggested those names to her Aunt and Uncle and was so pleased when they chose them and also when they named their newly built house in Stakesby Vale, 'Dololee', a compilation of the three names! Uncle John's offspring were called Bernard, Dennis, Fiona and Jean, but I didn't see much of them either; as I said, they were all older than me but my brother was quite friendly with them until they all married and moved away.

All four family houses were within the same square mile and within easy striking, well, walking, distance of each other, and Havelock Place was a large corner house at the end of Abbey Terrace, with room enough for my mother and grandfather, so that's where they went.

This must have been a very difficult time for Vee, having to move from a small, close, loving family, still grieving and missing her mother and siblings, to a larger, colder house and atmosphere where her elderly grandparents and two aunts were very strict, expecting her to share the work of the house, run errands and I guess not treating her with as much love and understanding as she had been used to. I don't want to imply they were unkind to her or anything, but times were hard and the situation would be different to what she had been used to. Vee was still attending school and studying piano and I think that having to accept things as they were and adjust to it all, however sad and tough, probably helped to shape her character and motivate her to become the strong, bright, fun person who was to become my lovely 'Mums' – so I was very lucky there, wasn't I?

I mentioned that Vee was studying piano. Most people then did learn to play an instrument or to sing and her father, William Kidd, known among family and friends as W.K., not only sang but also led the local Bohemian Male Voice Choir – which together with the Amateur Dramatic Society was formed when a local music theatre called 'The Thespians' folded. By the time she was sixteen years old, having been encouraged by her father to spend hours practising for her music exams before and after school, Vee was a good enough pianist to accompany the choir during practice sessions and also when they performed. I can imagine how this would brighten her life quite a bit, providing a chance to wear her Sunday dress, get out of the house and no doubt chat to the young men in the choir.

So, time to introduce the man who was to become my Father, whose name, it's also time I told you, was Leonard, always called Leonard. I never, ever heard anyone call him Len. As I've already told you, Leonard and his mother had moved to the town from York, or thereabouts after losing his father and older brother. He himself had served in The Royal Flying Corps, later the RAF, during the war; but just before that he had started studying accountancy so after arriving and settling in their new home he joined a local firm of Accountants and continued to work towards his final qualification. He was also interested in music and had a good baritone voice, so of course (guess what!) he joined the local Male Voice Choir. He was 24 years old and unattached and of course I have no idea whether he had any previous romance in his life, I just know he fell a bundle for the pretty fair haired daughter of his choirmaster who was then only sixteen. So it would be a year of the odd chatting at rehearsals before he approached W.K. for permission to ask her out, because, as you may or may not know, that's how it was done in those days.

At Havelock Place where Vee and W.K. now lived, one of her two Aunts, Nan, was 'courting' a man called Bert who was temporarily working in the town and had (well obviously) survived his army war service. They were married about this time and moved to live in the London area and will come back into my story later. The other aunt, Sarah, called Sally, was a seamstress and worked for the main fashion house in the town.

About the time my Father began courting my Mother she had started working in the same shipping office in the town as W.K. Everyone walked to where they needed to be; very few people owned a car and even bicycles were a bit of a luxury.

The house was, as I've said, near the top of the west cliff and the office where they both worked was situated at the bottom, near the harbour and quayside, not so bad going down but several steep hills on the way back. I'm telling you this because one evening, during their homeward climb after a long day's work, W.K. suffered a severe stroke, causing quite a commotion as you can imagine. He was then confined to a wheelchair but eventually bedridden and looked after mostly by Vee until he sadly died in the year 1919.

Vee was then 17 years old and as she was now left without any of her immediate family she must have truly welcomed Leonard's interest in her. In October 1921 she and my father were married in the village of Holmwood near London in Surrey. I believe that was where her older brother Alan had settled and as Leonard was the proud owner of a motorbike and sidecar, believe it or not that was how they travelled from North Yorkshire to London for the wedding – no easy journey by any means in those days. I have no idea why they didn't get married in Whitby. As I've already said, we didn't talk about things like that, but I can imagine it was a very low key affair with only her brother's family attending and I rather think a few days in London would be their only honeymoon.

Nevertheless, returning home to settle in with Grandma Nell at Whitehaven, Vee's life was much improved. Her great sadness at losing her mother, the illness and death of her father only five years later was eased by the way she was loved and welcomed into her new home. Her mother-in-law was happy for Leonard to have found someone to love and was kind and helpful to Vee, encouraging and guiding the new young wife, particularly when, within a few months, she became pregnant and had their son, my brother Peter in August 1922.

They remained at Whitehaven, happily I believe, for the next few years until after I came along. It was, and still is a pleasant house, stone built, painted white, double fronted, on the corner of two wide tree-lined avenues and large enough for us all to live comfortably I would have thought. However, shortly after I was born, they moved as I have said to the aforementioned Church Square. I can only think the move was for financial reasons because they didn't just buy the one house, No 4, but the one next door to it as well, No. 5, living in one and renting out the other during the summer months. This makes a lot of sense I suppose in view of a growing family and my father the sole provider, particularly as seaside holidays were then fast becoming popular and the town was blessed with three miles of sandy beach with the vast north sea to sail on or splash about in and for those from the industrial areas a chance to just breathe in the fresh salty air.

Anyway, here I am, I've arrived! My earliest memory is of being put on a large bed next to a lady lying in the bed propped up on pillows who must have been my Grandma Nell shortly before she passed away. It's rather strange that I remember this so clearly, for I was probably only about 18 months old and don't remember anything else around this time; and although she must have been very ill and dying, the image hasn't stayed with me as an unpleasant one. This is my only memory of my Grandma who I believe was a kind and good person and whose love has somehow stayed with me when she could not.

With all four Grandparents by then having passed away the only extended family I now had was the Uncle in London, Alan, who I never met, the two Great Grand Parents and Great Aunt Sally, the seamstress at Havelock Place, Nan and her family in London, two Great Uncles, Arthur and John and their families, who I hardly ever saw, and Great Aunt Esther in New Zealand who I've already mentioned I never met. There were some cousins of Leonard's scattered about who I did briefly come into contact with when they came to stay with us but I must say, although it sounds like a large family, it didn't seem so. Then eventually there was Aunt Alice, Grandma Nell's sister who at some point came to live with us – I'll tell you about her later. Well, that's it for now, so on to the next part.

Chapter 2

Age Nothing to Five

OF THE FIRST FEW YEARS of my life I have no memory, other than the one I've already mentioned about my Grandma Nell. So there are only a few things I can say about that time based on what I was told later on. There was a lot going on. Women had earned the right to vote in political elections after a few brave ones called the Suffragettes protested in various ways at the injustice of them being treated as second class citizens, without the intelligence to decide who should represent them in making the laws of the land. This led to more campaigning for women to gain equal rights with men in other things, at least in our country. Young people like Leonard and Vee were responding to these changes and were very much a part of it, but for the older generation used to firmer controls it must have seemed worrying.

By the time I became slightly aware of the world outside the small circle of life around me, like most people I suppose, I just accepted it all and knew I was safe enough and fortunate. I don't think we were rich, moneywise, but I didn't feel deprived in any way and it seemed like we had all we needed and I felt loved and cared for.

The other house next door to where we then lived in Church Square was actually a small private school which must have seemed to my parents the obvious place to start my education. It was in September 1930 then that I embarked on learning the three R's. I was four and a half years old and small for my age. The uniform of the school was a dark brown tunic, cream coloured blouse, dark brown stockings and a brown hat shaped like a pork pie (yes, honestly). The tunics were handmade and Mums told me once that mine was evidently the smallest they had ever had to make which for some reason, or maybe it was just the way she said it, caused me to feel somehow special. I suppose it was knowing my Mums seemed pleased with me about something that gave me an early confidence booster which nevertheless often wavered later on because I was certainly never allowed to act big-headed about anything. Showing off was just not acceptable, being modest was. Anyway I was 4 years old, small for my age and starting school in the smallest tunic they had ever made!

Time to move on.

It's now 1930. My Grandma has died and because Daddy's older brother Earnest had been killed in the war, it meant that he, my Daddy, was the sole beneficiary of her will. Although he was still working and also studying for his final accountancy exams he and Mums decided to be very adventurous and use the inheritance to buy a plot of land immediately behind our houses in Church Square which was closer to the cliffs and sea, and to build a hotel there. Tourism was growing and the little seaside town was gaining popularity with its rich history and ancient charm. I'm sure they also hoped the brave venture would build financial security for us, so the Church Square houses were put on the market to be sold.

Leonard had a cousin, Raymond, who was an Architect and lived only about 20 miles away in Scarborough, so it was natural I suppose that he was called upon to draw up plans for the proposed building, which he did, and planning permission was obtained for a 35-bedroom hotel. The plot of land was purchased from the local council who had taken it over from a developer called George Hudson who had over-stretched himself financially and couldn't complete the partly built Royal Crescent; eventually the area was bought by Sir George Elliot who built the Spa Complex but did not complete the crescent and sold out to the council who eventually sold it to us. So it was sad in a way that the terrace would not be completed but this was a time of economic breakdown and any building for potential growth and future employment was to be welcomed, and so it was that the project was given the go-ahead.

Building work eventually began and, if you can imagine, it was only yards from the rear of our then home in Church Square so we could watch it grow. I sometimes think of the stresses my parents must have suffered though during the months of construction followed by the equipping and furnishing, advertising, staffing and then planning the catering for anything up to 50 people, what a task! I'm sure that first year must have been a very worrying learning curve and would also be the beginning of a rather unusual lifestyle which I would be a part of – my home yes, but one which was also a seasonal business with one way of life from Easter to October and a completely different life from October to March.

Chapter 3

Home is a Hotel

I DON'T REMEMBER anything about the move but I expect, unlike my parents, I would find it fun and exciting, loads of space to run around in, two staircases to run up and down, 35 bedrooms to explore and many windows to gaze out from. Cousin Raymond had designed the building so that every letting room had a full or partial sea view; after all, that's what future visitors, many escaping from their industrial cities would mainly be coming for, and it's what I also came to love – to see every day that wide expanse of ocean in all its moods and to imagine what lay beyond especially when ships sailed by and then disappeared beyond the horizon

The style of the building was Georgian, brick built and with long sash windows. There was a central column with a glazed porch entrance leading into the large reception hall which had two wings at each side, one housing the dining room and the other the residents lounge. Cloakrooms and Daddy's office-cum-Reception were at the rear of the hall and the wide staircase led up to the three floors. There was a lovely stained glass window on the first landing which blocked out the view of the rear entrance and parking area. Staff, business and catering areas were also at the back as you would expect. It was an imposing structure but of course in complete contrast to the Edwardian architecture of the existing crescent of houses opposite; however, it was a hotel and needed to look like one and to have its own identity. I have no doubt that there would be plenty of local gossip and complaints about it at the time and since, such as: 'They should (!) have completed the crescent!' or, 'It doesn't look right!' etc.

They named it the Hotel Princess Royal after the daughter of King George V and Queen Mary who were our sovereigns at the time. Grandma Nell had earlier donated money towards the building of the new cottage hospital in the town which the Princess Royal had recently ceremoniously opened, so my parents thought, perhaps over-ambitiously, to invite her to do the same for our hotel which was after all, to be in her name. Needless to say the dear lady had more important things to do and politely declined. However she did marry a Yorkshireman, the Lord Lascelles and lived her life within the county at Harewood House, near Leeds. Neither Leonard nor Vee had any training or experience of the catering business yet they must have had a natural insight into what was needed because from the outset it seemed to me that everything ran smoothly and efficiently. There may have been an element of luck but they had obviously done plenty of research and much planning, especially in choosing efficient, loyal and enthusiastic people to work for and with them.

In 1930 the country was still suffering from The Depression remember, so jobs were still scarce. The four most important positions, apart from my parents who were the resident, working proprietors, were Chef, Housekeeper, Head Waitress and Hall Porter. The Chef they chose was very experienced and affable and came with his wife, also much experienced, who became the head waitress. They had both worked on cruise ships and in major hotels and they proved to be an excellent choice becoming a reliable link between my parents and the rest of the staff. Their names were Alf and Flo but of course Alf was always called Chef. He was tall and rather handsome. Flo was also tall and although a bit stern-looking, had a great personality and the rest of the staff knew not to argue with her; she was the uncrowned 'head of state' as it were, but she ruled with kindness and humour and almost gushing attentiveness to the guests, who, she was well aware, could be generous with their tips.

The first Housekeeper who reigned supreme from the Linen Room on the first floor was called Mrs Berry. I never knew her first name – I called her Mrs B. She lived locally and had a daughter called Sheila who went to my school and became a friend. She was responsible for keeping everything upstairs spotless and smooth-running, two Chambermaids being under her wing. Then there was the Hall Porter, George; he was also a local man and his wife Lily helped out occasionally at the busiest times such as Bank and school holidays and the Regatta weekend. Their teenage daughter Elsie had the dubious task of looking after me during school Summer holidays when my parents were obviously otherwise engaged, this was only for the first two seasons though, when I would be 5 or 6 years old; after that I was perfectly able to move around town on my own or with school friends, with plenty of freedom to explore and get to know and to love the square half-mile in which I was growing up.

While we're on the subject, I want to tell you more about the people who came to work at the hotel and who became virtually my extended family and I still remember them all with great affection all these years later. In the Dining Room, under the firm rule of Flo, there was Theresa, pretty and dark haired and Marian, who was fair and petite and always seemed to be smiling. They both came from the industrial part of North Yorkshire now re-named Cleveland, and used to say how they loved coming to the seaside and the fresh air, away from all the factories and smoke. These two were already friends when they arrived, and elected to stay on during the winters to look after us, which was great.

When my parents went away for a few days in October for a well-deserved break, Terry, as we called Theresa, and Marian were there to take care of me. By this time my brother was away at boarding school and I certainly did feel special with the huge building all to myself and my two kind 'minders'. They would take it in turns to have a day off and both somehow managed to acquire boyfriends in the town on which subject I became very interested and would pressure them continually for news of how they were getting on. Looking back I realise how fortunate I was to have the occasional care of these two who treated my curiosity with patience and good humour, never telling me to 'be quiet' or 'go away' yet only giving me as much information as I could understand. I think it was the start of my learning that having a romance was part of being grown up and it sounded really nice and something to look forward to.

In the kitchen Louise (Louie), a lovely local lass, was chef's assistant who did all the major washing up and clearing away after each meal. She was very plump and jolly and always had a smile on her face. She could be quite cheeky in a fun way, but very kind, and I loved having a sly joke with her. There were huge ovens and sinks in the kitchen but no dishwashers then so extra help would be called in during the height of the season. Then there was the 'still room' between the kitchen and dining room where the serving up took place and where my mother took charge at every meal, plating, checking and serving up to the waitresses from behind the warming ovens and hot plate, supported by Mrs B. and of course Chef, who would bring the freshly cooked food from the kitchen as required. It was hot work – in my mind I can still see Mums pausing to wipe her brow and take a breath, yet smiling because I suppose she felt pleased to be making sure everything went smoothly. The stillroom was also where the light crockery and silverware was washed, dried and put away ready for the next session and where the large 'fridge' lived. I don't remember there being a deep freezer; in the 1930's they were not in common use like a lot of other things which today are taken for granted. Everything was purchased locally and cooked freshly as needed. Jenny was the 'stillroom maid' who, as quietly as she could, cleared the used dishes as they were brought out of the dining room and who had a sort of light hearted but respectful camaraderie with Mums and Chef which just seemed to be part of the way it all came together and worked, a happy atmosphere in spite of the intensity at mealtimes – which were at specific times, Breakfast at nine, Lunch at one and Dinner at seven. A gong located at the top of the first flight of stairs would be struck on the dot at each time. Sometimes I would be allowed to bang the gong which was great! Afternoon Tea was served at four and everything, a week's accommodation, all meals included, was to be had for a pre-war price of £4.50. We'd be lucky to get a coffee and a piece of cake for that amount these days, wouldn't we?

As you can imagine, in the really busy times I learnt to keep away from all this activity and wait until things calmed down before venturing through the kitchen to the stillroom for my own meal. I loved this – Mums always greeted me with a little joke such as 'Now what would Madam like today?' or 'Ah! Here comes our most important customer' – but in spite of all the delicious food on offer, I was a faddy eater and usually chose the simplest things such as Chef's home-made cold meats and maybe a steamed pudding or often just a banana.

After each meal all the staff would sit around a large table in the kitchen and have a good 'tuck in' with lots of chat and laughter. They did have their arguments sometimes but it seemed to me that anything would soon be sorted out by Chef or Mums, who was always referred to as 'madam,' or perhaps by my peace-loving father, 'sir', who although he was mostly at 'front of house' in his office, he would be the bearer of the weekly wages, little buff envelopes distributed every Friday and shoved into apron pockets under smiling faces. Daddy would have a cheery word with each of them, keeping in touch and in his quiet way letting each employee know they were valued.

It was common knowledge that the staff members who lived locally always came with large bags and took food home with them at the end of the working day, but no-one, including my folks seemed to notice or care; the atmosphere was sort of 'give and take' and I think it was just accepted as a perk of the job.

Cousin Raymond's plans had not included any separate accommodation for us the family, except for one very small living/dining room next to the main kitchen plus a large family bedroom on the third (top) floor which we all shared in the summer until my brother was thought too old to share with us and had his own top floor room. I didn't understand why this had to happen and missed him at first but I liked being in with Mums and Daddy which was just as well really because by the time I too was old enough to have my own room Adolph Hitler was knocking on everyone's door, except of course he didn't knock, did he? He and his army marched in uninvited all over Europe and our lives changed – more of that later.

There was, of course, a back staircase with access to each floor and where Chef and Flo had their own tiny room. On the top floor there was a large dormitory near our family room, for the live-in female staff. This arrangement seemed to work, as my parents being 'hands on' and much at the heart of everything, well, it was like one big working family and I was in the middle of it all and I loved it, even though I knew it was a bit strange and not how my friends lived.

Of course because Whitby at that time was strictly a seasonal resort, at the end of September everything changed. During October the staff began to drift away with just the local staff members staying on to clean, put things away and close up for the winter. We moved down to bedrooms on the first floor but still used the same small living room which had an open fire; it would have been uneconomical to attempt to heat and use the main hotel rooms and, anyway, our little room was certainly cosy and was the beginning of the totally different lifestyle we had in the winter.

Chapter 4

Early Thoughts

I'M PRETTY SURE my father thought of himself as far from perfect, but to me he was. In appearance I suppose he was rather 'Dickensian' looking. Not very tall and neither slim nor overweight, to me he was just cuddly. I remember sometimes I would curl up on his knee as we listened to what is now called the radio but which we then called the wireless, and I still remember the warm feeling I had of belonging and safety. His hair was straight and dark until it turned silver prematurely and he wore it brushed back very neatly, short back and sides being the usual style for most men then. He was always clean shaven with a healthy complexion and the softest, kindest hazel eyes which often twinkled. Although I guessed he found it hard to say 'no' to me, he occasionally did, and I knew it would be useless to plead or to badger him. I don't remember that he ever lost his temper and his wry sense of humour and gentle manner got him through most of life's problems, except one.

Daddy's left leg was diseased with a condition called Osteomyelitis which no doctor seemed to be able to do anything about. He never complained or moaned about it but occasionally I would see him wince in obvious pain and he would rub his leg and ask me to pass him a foot stool to rest it on. I think over time, I just accepted the 'bad leg' as a part of him but I did once ask him about it and he blamed himself, saying he was sure it was the result of once having sat on wet grass and he made me promise never to sit on anything wet or damp and I don't think I ever have.

Before the leg got really bad Daddy's main recreation was golf so he was a member of the local club and in the winter months played regularly. Even in summer after lunch when the hotel guests were out doing what guests do, he would snatch a couple of hours and play 9 holes to keep on top of his game, as they say. He was a popular member and served as Captain one year but eventually the leg stopped him being able to manage even 9 holes and even walking in the countryside which he loved, also became difficult. Life can be very unfair.

Daddy, being an Accountant, ran the business side of things from his office. It was situated off the hall and had a sliding window from where he dealt with client enquiries, payments and communicating with George the porter. Then there was the daily post, enquiries and reservations to deal with, balancing the books and, long before computers were even thought of, all the correspondence to be typed or, failing that, with pen and ink; even the revolutionary Biro was yet to appear.

About my Mums, well I did put her on a bit of a pedestal too, as she seemed to be good at just about everything; of course she couldn't have been, but I always felt that if things went horribly wrong she would know what to do about it. Like Daddy, she had a strong value system and made sure I was polite and behaved myself but she also had a great sense of humour and enjoyment of life. There's no question, that at times just a look from her, especially in adult company, was enough to stop me saying or doing something that might be embarrassing; so I suppose I became a bit unsure of myself, nervous in adult company and learnt mostly to keep my mouth shut; but hey! no-one's upbringing is perfect and anyway when I was with my friends I had plenty to say for myself.

She, my Mums, was small, about 5ft 2ins tall, with fair curly hair and very blue eyes. She was definitely into fashion and always dressed smartly, and, I thought, more up to date than her friends, some of whom were quite a bit older than her. She seemed to have loads of energy which was just as well, in the summer at least, as she was always on the go and you had to be quick to catch up with her.

After serving breakfast, Mums and Mrs B. would sit down in the family room and have their meal. Daddy and I would have had ours and departed, he to his office-cum reception and me, between the Easter and summer holidays, back to school. After breakfast Mums met with Chef to discuss the day's menus, deciding what needed to be ordered and delivered. Once that was done the handwritten menus were passed to Daddy to be typed up and then given to Flo for the Dining Room. Mums had her strict routine. After the meeting with Chef, she would telephone orders to be delivered, but would usually walk down the hills into town to pick up things like flowers and small items. We did have a car – I think it was a Hillman but I could be wrong. Mums didn't drive, not many people did and anyway I think she liked to keep in touch with the local shopkeepers and probably meet and have a quick chat with a friend or two on the way. One thing I know Mums did after serving the lunch and having had her own: she would disappear for a quick nap and was not to be disturbed, usually for about an hour which was probably a life-saving exercise as she would then be on the go again overseeing everything until late.

Did Daddy and Mums ever have a falling-out? Yes, of course they did, and it was a nerve-racking time for me, especially after I started going to the 'pictures' and learnt there was such a thing as 'divorce'. What happened was that Mums would stop speaking to Daddy so you knew she was displeased with him about something although it was never obvious what that was! Daddy would keep trying to 'break the ice' but it didn't usually work and sometimes she would ask me to answer for her as in 'tell your father so and so' which was quite funny if it hadn't been so worrying. Anyway eventually, usually after one or two days, things were back to normal and I used to breathe a sigh of relief. One thing parents don't seem to realise is how much their children can worry about them.

On the whole I believe my parents were a very good partnership and really cared for each other but it's unrealistic to think everything and every day is perfect. People have moods and bad days and sometimes their ideas clash, especially when they work together as mine did. I think that although I knew this I had a fear of losing them in some way, but because most of the time they seemed to be happy with each other and their lot, I suppose I learnt how to be happy with my lot and accept there would always be good days and bad but at this point I knew I had very little to be unhappy about.

By the time I was eight years old I was used to my summer/winter lifestyles. Summer started when two or more of the local staff returned to begin the opening-up routine. Carpets were rolled up (none of the carpets were fitted as few were then) and carried out onto the adjacent Tuckers Field to be beaten and shaken free of any dust; the beaters were shaped like a tennis racquet but very light and bendy. Windows were opened wide and washed inside and out; the girls would actually sit on the window ledge to do the outside panes and I would be so worried they would fall out, especially when they were doing the upstairs bedroom ones – thankfully no-one ever did. Mattresses were turned and aired and beds made up; in fact, every available inch was cleaned and polished and everything that had been packed or stacked away in the autumn was returned to its summer place. I thought all the hustle and bustle was exciting after the closed-up winter months and would run around chatting to them all when I got home from school.

The little private school I had been going to had moved to a larger building about half a mile away and my walk there took me past Ledbury, the house where my mother had lived on Crescent Avenue, and then passed Whitehaven where I had been born; then I would usually meet my classmates coming from Upgang Lane and we'd walk or run the rest of the way down Chubb Hill. We were there for nine, home for lunch at 12:30, back to school for 2 p.m. and home again at 4. There was no being dropped off by car or picked up in those days whatever the weather, and believe me on the north-east coast of Yorkshire it can be rough.

The school was called Hildathorpe and was very different from the educational system of today. First of all it was mainly for girls, although boys could attend up to age 9 or 10, after which they were off to the boys-only school run by the council, or the revolutionary Secondary Modern or the Grammar School or some, like my brother, went away to boarding school. The Headmistress was called Mrs Caithness and the 'second in command' was Miss Shegog who was her niece. Caithy, as we not very imaginatively called the Head, was rather severe-looking and although she was probably only in her fifties we considered her to be very ancient. She had dark grey wavy hair always worn in a neat bun at the back of her head. She had steel-rimmed glasses and her mouth seemed always to be sort-of pursed, if you know what I mean, as though in a constant state of disapproval or like she'd just eaten something sour. Somehow we all knew we'd better behave, or else! Oh yes, and her back was always ramrod straight and she tried to make sure ours were too: 'Head up, shoulders back, stop slouching!'

Miss Shegog, (Gogs) on the other hand had a twinkle in her eye; you felt she really liked children and enjoyed teaching. Her main subject was English and she instilled in me an interest in our language by making it fun and interesting so that a love of words has stayed with me. Even out of class, if we said anything ungrammatical, or just sloppy, we would be corrected; if, for instance, I said 'Please Miss Shegog, can I leave the room?' a sharp retort would come: 'I expect you CAN, but whether you MAY is a different matter!' Also, any mispronounced words would be corrected; we certainly would never have got away with using 'f' instead of 'th' as many do today as in 'nuffin for 'nothing' or adding a 'k' as in 'nothingk', or even worse, 'nuffingk'. Of course, we didn't have computers or even adding machines and even if we'd had mobile phones they certainly wouldn't have been allowed within a mile of the school; but we did learn how to speak correctly and clearly and to work things out for ourselves, and Gogs had a sense of humour and used it to keep our attention – and it worked for me. My father added to this by buying classic children's books for me on birthdays or Christmas, such as *Black Beauty, Little Women, Treasure Island,* and by enjoying reading himself and encouraging me to go to the library where I remember getting *'Just William'* books. Maths subjects, Geography and History, didn't interest me and I struggled in those exams, but reading opened up a whole new world beyond my cosy small town one and stretched my mind to life's possibilities and challenges. My other interests were dancing – oh boy, how I loved to dance! Also, Gym (P.E.) and Netball were favourites. So you can guess I wasn't destined for the academic world, but then very few girls were back in the 'Thirties'.

The school was a double-fronted Victorian building similar to many built as the town had developed. They had had a separate extension built at the rear which housed the two middle forms, (they were not called 'classes' then); Kindergarten (reception) and the first form were in the main building, forms 2 and 3 were in the extension, then it was back to the main house to forms 4 and 5 where it was hoped a school-leaving certificate, the School Cert as it was called, would be gained.

There was no playground. In the few minutes between classes we just relaxed a bit, chatted and giggled, and in Winter we would gather round the huge stove in the middle of the room – no central heating then! It was pretty strict, I suppose. School was for learning, not playing – but we didn't mind; it was a break and we could chat legitimately which we weren't allowed to do in class, oh my word no! There was a sixth form but hardly anyone stayed there long enough to move into it and gain what was called the Higher Cert. Each form had no more than ten pupils; some had less and we sat in rows behind desks or tables so it was difficult to get away with not paying attention or cribbing or anything else. I know how different things are nowadays, but Hildathorpe was the school I went to until I was 15 years old and where I was happy, had good friends and got a very good basic education, even though I did do a lot of day-dreaming through the boring bits.

Chapter 5

How It Was (or Had To Be)

THE HOTEL OPENED for business just before Easter but the preparations, as I've already said, would have started some three to four weeks earlier. After the first two years I was well used to the annual springtime routine of moving up to the top floor family bedroom, the staff members returning and all the activity of making the place ready for action once more. Although I don't think I felt restricted in any way I learnt that once the guests arrived, I no longer had the run of the whole building. I knew my boundaries and knew I was not to 'bother the staff' when they were busy or 'get in the way' of anyone or anything. I remember I went through a period of being desperate to have a pet, preferably a dog, and from time to time I would plead with Mums or Daddy to get one but was told very firmly that it was out of the question with lots of reasons, mostly to do with the running of the hotel, so I eventually gave up. Down town by the quayside, there was a pet shop opposite the Railway Station and sometimes at weekends, I would take myself there and just wander around gazing longingly at the pets for sale and breathe in the lovely smells, pretending I was there to choose a puppy; well, that was the nearest I got then to having a pet.

I suppose I learnt early on that you can't have everything you want in life and that there are priorities. Our home was also our business and hopefully paid for our needs and the bills, and although my parents were very occupied in the summer, they were always there and available to me and I felt very much a part of it all and not in any way neglected or deprived. Then in most of the winter months we were very much more together and relaxed, so having a pet you see was a want, not a need and I guess I had all the needs. I can see now that my parents were right to be firm with me when I asked to have a dog, as I then knew not to have false hopes; of course I didn't understand that then but realise now they were right.

At the front of the hotel there was a parking area for about five cars bordered by a low wall and flower beds. To one side was a grassed area facing the sea and where guests could sit outside, and on the other side a driveway leading to a parking and utility area and the rear entrance for deliveries and the staff and in the summertime for our friends and ourselves as well, although even in winter we would usually use this way in and out as it was more sheltered than the front which faced the sea and the winter winds. Daddy wanted to grow Ivy on the walls at the front to soften the bare brickwork, but 'Ivy' obviously couldn't cope with the cold North Sea gales and after several attempts I think he gave up on 'her'! The road in front formed part of the semi-circular crescent and was only a few yards from the promenade and cliff side and the area between the two was laid out with wide lawns and flower beds and it was called the Crescent Gardens. There were pathways and benches to sit on and all just across the road from the hotel so I would often pop over there, wander about at will and think of it as the garden of my palace where of course I was a Princess. I had a wild imagination and if no-one was about I'd be having all sorts of conversations with kings, queens, the Prime Minister, Robin Hood, you name it, sorting out the country, giving orders to my troops, you know, that sort of thing.

Across the promenade from Crescent Gardens, and also only yards from the hotel there was a gateway through to steps which led down the cliff side to a complex of wonderful buildings called The Spa and from where there were more steps to the beach. The main building there was the Pavilion and each summer season it became home to a symphony orchestra which played both classical and popular music each evening. There was an open walkway around the upper glazed part of the building where people could sit outside if they chose, weather permitting, and enjoy the music through the open windows and watch the sunset. Adjacent to the orchestra area there was a café where my parents would sometimes manage to pop down and meet their friends in the evening after their duties in the hotel were done; it was a way they could keep in touch with their friends during the summer. Also in the complex there was a theatre where a concert party would perform in the early evenings for the main part of the season and when that entertainment ended the floor would be cleared and a live dance band appear for ballroom dancing. The Spa complex really was a magical place, built as it was into the cliff side and open to wide views of the sea, the coastline and the summer evening sunsets.

Much of my summer school holidays were spent in or around the Spa. My birthday is in May and the year I was nine, Daddy's gift to me was a Spa season ticket which allowed me free entrance to The Spa and all its activities. It also gave me a quick way down to the beach. The cost of the ticket was ten shillings, about 50p in today's money. In 1935, ten shillings was a weekly wage for many people; it would pay the rent and cover basic needs. How things have changed! Wages may have increased but so have prices and I think that even then when I took so much for granted, I knew my season ticket was a special gift.

My Uncle Bert and Aunt Nan, who had left the town to live in London, had three children, two girls and a boy. Audrey, the eldest, was six years older than me and so was closer to my brother and even my Mums. She didn't seem interested in me at all; well, I suppose to her I was too young and boring. Harry was about the same age as Peter my brother so they were great buddies and then there was Betty, three years older than me who became like the older sister I didn't have. Every school holiday the family returned to stay at the house in Havelock Place where Aunt Sarah, the only unmarried one, still lived and who made clothes for local people on her magnificent sewing machine.

So at the beginning of every holiday Peter and I would wait expectantly and excitedly for our cousins to arrive and on the day they were due kept asking if we could go and see them, like: 'Will they be here yet?' 'How long does it take from London?' or 'Is it time?' or 'Can we go down now?' Eventually we'd be given the go-ahead, would race out of the house, okay, hotel, round the corner and down the hill and burst in on them all with whoops of joy. Although Peter and I both had our local friends, getting together with our cousins in the school holidays was a regular ritual.

Once Peter and Harry were reunited they were inseparable. Sometimes they would meet up with other local lads, either for a game of football on the beach, hanging around the town and fish quay, or if they could scrounge enough money from parents, going to 'the pictures'. Betty, or 'Bets', as I called her, would meet up with the daughter of friends of our parents, who was the same age as Bets and her name was Margaret; but I never once heard her called that – she was always 'Midge'. I was lucky that Bets and Midge usually let me tag along with them, which I did as often as I could, especially in the summer.

Uncle Bert, who I knew had an important job in London, drove the family up but was only able to stay for about two weeks; then he would go back South until it was time to come and take them home. However for the summer he rented a large hut for us all down on the sea wall which bordered the beach. This was a wonderful place for us kids to meet, change into and out of our swimsuits, shelter from the rain, have picnics and just enjoy the summer. About once or twice a week Mums and Aunt Nan would come down to the hut for an hour or two in the afternoon bringing cakes and other goodies. Since Daddy and Mums had married, Nan and Mums, although they were Aunt and Niece and were ten years apart in age, had become good friends and when they were together they were like a pair of comedians. They would pretend to be canteen ladies with broad Yorkshire accents and have us kids in fits of giggles. Bets and Midge and I would try to do the same when they weren't there but we were no match for our Mums. Daddy didn't 'do' the beach. I only remember him being there once and he obviously wasn't comfortable; apart from having the bad leg, it seemed definitely out of his comfort zone and I knew if he had a spare hour or so he would be happier spending time in the country or on the golf course.

The two or three years before I was old enough to go to the Spa in the evenings, I would be sent up to bed in the big top floor family bedroom. I would climb into bed and watch Mums getting ready to go out with Daddy, either to the Spa or the Golf Club where they met up with their friends most of who also had businesses in the town. As I've said, Mums had moved with the times and used make-up and I loved to watch her putting lipstick on and doing her hair. It was very basic then, no moisturiser or base and definitely no eye make-up – that was considered going too far and reserved for acting on stage with the local Am-Drams in the winter. Of course they had no need of a babysitter for me as there was always someone on duty in the evenings for the hotel guests. After my parents had gone though, I suppose I did sometimes feel a bit lonely, and not at all tired. There were two dormer windows, and as one of them faced the sea-front and crescent, I would climb onto a chair and watch the people strolling by below and make up stories about them in my head. During August I would see the fishing fleet sailing out to sea from the harbour mouth to catch the herring overnight; the boats would all have their lights on and it was an amazing sight, like a brightly lit village moving slowly away.

One night, I suppose I was a bit bored and put a chair in front of the mirror, I found a pair of scissors and cut my hair. I soon realised it wasn't an improvement. In fact, it was a horrible mess and although I made sure my head was under the covers when my parents came in, the next morning the ugly truth was there for all to see. No-one made much of a fuss – I was just hauled along to the hairdresser who did what she could with the remaining bits of hair and I had to put up with it looking odd for ages. Maybe a psychologist might say it was an act of rebellion at being on my own. I don't think so but who knows! Anyway, I didn't ever do it again and have a great respect for hairdressers.

I think I was nine when I first went to the pictures, cinema or movies as they're called now. It was to the first full length animated Disney film 'Snow White and the Seven Dwarfs'. By then, 1935, the original silent films had developed soundtrack and had become the 'Talkies' and although they were still in black and white, it was believed they would soon be made in colour as well which they soon were with the arrival of the fabulous musicals. Hollywood, a suburb of Los Angeles in America, was becoming the main producer of this exciting new medium and a whole new entertainment industry was developing and showing ordinary people a wider, different and a more glamorous way of life, so entertaining in the home gradually became less important. Anyway at nine years old I accepted the magic of the movies much as young people today accept television or the computer.

At first, I was only allowed to go to cartoon films like Popeye or Mickey Mouse but I soon graduated to the musicals with the singing and dancing of Fred Astaire and Ginger Rogers, or teenage comedies with Mickey Rooney and Judy

Garland and Deanna Durbin, who had a beautiful singing voice. Films were being made in London too, comedies or historical ones. Mostly I would go with Bets, or Bets and her friend Midge, and if we could manage it, at least once a week. During the more sophisticated stories I would keep whispering to Bets to explain certain things I didn't understand, and she would get pretty annoyed, 'shushing' me and saying she'd tell me later but she never did and I'd just forget anyway. There were three cinemas in the town – the Empire was the first, soon followed by a specially built, grander version called the Coliseum. The latter had huge satin curtains covering the screen which were lit by coloured lights from above and ceremoniously swept apart when the programme was about to begin. It was very impressive and exciting and going to the pictures was a magical experience for me.

A smaller much less glamorous version was located at the top of one of the alleyways which are a feature of the town and lead off from the main streets. It's official name was the Waterloo but it was universally referred to as 'the Flea Pit'; it was definitely not in the same class as the other two but if a film you wanted to see was on there then you had to brave the suspected fleas and go. The upstairs gallery felt like it was about to collapse at any moment and we were all amazed it never did. As well as the singing/dancing films with Astaire and Rogers I also loved the Western adventures which transported us into another strange but exciting world of galloping horses and cowboys and those early American pioneering days.

The more sophisticated films provided an insight into adventurous exploits, strange situations which generally caused me to think about the rest of the world and beyond my own rather narrow one. In spite of finding geography lessons dull, I liked seeing those far-off places on film which brought other places and history to life in an interesting, understandable way.

I also liked the Boy meets Girl stories and in those days they always had happy endings and the good guy won the nice girl and they married before even thinking of having a family. It was all good wholesome stuff and I think added to my general education and attitude to life and probably contributed to my being a committed romantic.

The year I turned 10 I became friendly with a new girl at school called Rosalind but we called her Roz. She was about a year younger than me. Her father was Frank Gomez and he was the conductor of the Symphony Orchestra at the Spa. Her mother had the position of first violin in the orchestra and I think her older brother was also a musician. They were only in Whitby for the summer season. I don't know where they went in the winter, I only know that Roz and I spent a lot of time together in the summer school holidays mostly in or around the Spa and whenever I wasn't tagging along with Bets and Midge, that is.

Shirley Temple was a very famous child film star at that time and Roz and I used to take turns in pretending to be her, singing, acting and dancing around, usually on the beach and we would make up our own stories. The trouble was that Roz was not only nearer in age to Shirley, she also looked very much like her with a mass of gorgeous light brown curly hair; my hair was straight and sort of ordinary brown, so I didn't feel very good when it was my turn to be her. Imagination is a great thing and I loved all the dancing around and pretending. Roz and I half-believed that one day we would be 'discovered' while we were singing and dancing and would be whisked off to Hollywood to be famous!

Sometimes we would manage to talk our way into the actual Pavilion when Roz's father was conducting the orchestra and if he spied us he would play 'The Teddy Bears' Picnic' or something and announce that it was for us which made us feel really special. Looking back on those days when I was aged between 7 and 12 they seemed like a lifetime, especially the long summer ones. They were sometimes active and sometimes relaxing, just running around, or skipping, throwing or bouncing a ball, reading, sitting in the sun, playing cards or board games in the beach hut if it rained and sometimes getting soaked dashing home in the rain and having to jump in a hot bath.

Apart from the steps through the Spa and down to the beach there was also a steep zigzag path which we sometimes ran up and down, and there was a lift which I refused to go on as I didn't trust it not to break down and thought I may be stranded in it for ever. It's still there and it still breaks down from time to time so I wasn't all that ridiculous. At times I took a very short cut to the beach which was straight down the cliff face; if Mums and Daddy had known they would have been horrified because it was very steep in parts, but I was sure-footed and also liked to stop and pick the wild flowers growing down the cliff sides undisturbed, and later press them between sheets of paper in a big heavy book.

A short way up the promenade from the hotel was an open-air sport and leisure ground consisting of tennis courts, a bowling green and a miniature golf course. In the school summer term, tennis was our only sport and so we used these courts; it was voluntary and held in the evening on Fridays. I was a very willing volunteer and of course only had to hop over the fence behind the hotel, pop across a patch of Tucker's Field and I was there. Miss Bowyer was the gym mistress and our name for her was Bowlegs which the dear lady obviously couldn't help but definitely did have; we liked her though, and although she was firm with us and stood no nonsense, she was jolly and I really enjoyed those tennis evenings, sometimes very short if it rained. In the winter term, the only sport we played was netball on Friday afternoons and we had a half mile to walk to the town sports field so of course if the weather was too bad it was cancelled and we had to have gym or exercises in the classroom instead. I must say, though, we all liked Friday afternoons as for the first hour we had Needlework which was easy and relaxed and we could chat to each other; then after lunch it was either Netball or Gym and home for the weekend – wonderful!

Chapter 6

Their Friends

I DON'T KNOW exactly when Aunt Alice came to live with us. She was Grandma Nell's sister who at some point Daddy had promised his Mum he would always look after but knowing my Daddy he would have anyway. As far as I was concerned Aunt Alice had always been there and she just seemed to fit in. I believe Grandma Nell had worried about her younger sister being unmarried and alone as she wasn't exactly the brightest one in the family but she certainly had at least one great character asset, she didn't interfere, cause any problems or voice any opinions: she kept herself to herself and I can now appreciate how wise that was. Once the hotel was up and running in the summer, Aunt Alice had a specific job: she was in charge of the salt, pepper and mustard sets for the dining room tables, checking them every mealtime and making sure they were all filled and clean. She took this very seriously and did the job with great concentration and efficiency and I expect she was paid accordingly although I know Daddy and Mums would make sure she had all she needed. Thinking about Aunt Alice now, I realise I just took her for granted and can't remember talking to her much at all, although I must have at times I suppose. She was anything but demanding, always sitting in the same chair in our little living room quietly reading with her magnifying glass in her long, dark coloured dresses; she had a sweet, gentle face but for the life of me I can't remember how she wore her hair. I do remember, occasionally, if I was really bored or lonely, knocking on her bedroom door and she would invite me in and produce a box of her Pontefract Cakes, little round pieces of liquorice which I came to like. She never seemed to get upset or complain about anything, although I now realise her life was very restricted as she never seemed to go out or have any friends. I suppose she must have been content with her lot and happy just to be a part of our family and our lives. I don't recall her ever seeming to be unhappy, annoyed or ill or needing any special attention, and she was anything but demanding.

Aunt Alice may not have been considered the brightest flower in the bunch but I believe there was wisdom in her graceful acceptance of things and even gratitude for what she had, not dwelling on what she may have missed. How I regret not spending more time with this lady who was my only true aunt, so many missed opportunities, for instance, to learn about my Grandma Nell, Daddy's early life, the family background, etc., but then we didn't do that then, did we? I suppose it would have been considered prying or too inquisitive, even rude; anyway, it's too late now.

At some time during these years my Great Grandparents (Mums' Grandparents) who lived at Havelock Place must have died. No-one told me, but one year they just were not there anymore. I hadn't had much to do with them anyway and sadly didn't really miss them. I can't remember even asking where they were, which does now seem a bit strange.

Mums and Daddy had quite a large circle of friends, either from their connection with golf or the local Amateur Dramatic Society which came to life in the winter months. Mums also liked to play Bridge although she claimed she wasn't very good and Daddy had his Men's Club where he liked to meet up with his pals and have a game of Snooker. I called their close friends Aunty or Uncle even though they were not my true relatives; it was how I thought of them – they were too close to be called "Mr and Mrs" and Christian names would have been far too familiar. Mums' closest friend was Dorothy who she had known right through their schooldays and who hadn't married; she was my Godmother and I called her Auntie Doff. One Christmas, her gift to me I remember was a wristwatch, my first, which I treasured and of course had to wind up every night.

Auntie Doff lived with her Father and Brother Jack above the Family's Wine and Spirit Merchants shop which she managed and which was located on the quayside, right opposite the bridge. Sometimes in the winter I would go with Mums right down the three hills to Auntie Doffs and sit on a high chair in the office looking out of the window onto the quay watching all the people passing by while Mums and Auntie Doff chattered away. I imagined that if you could sit there for a whole week, you would see everyone in town pass by.

Other friends were Reg and Win, who were Midge's parents and owned and ran a local Bakery in the town. They also had a large Café and Ballroom which was used for wedding receptions and other celebrations including regular weekly dances as ballroom dancing had become so popular. Reg was tall and bald and I suppose 'jocular' would describe his personality in spite of having to be up so early every day and work so hard, which bakers do; also, he was a golfer like Daddy and they all used to get involved with the Am Drams when there was a play on the go which was in the Autumn or early Spring when everyone was free to help or take part. They were all mostly about Daddy's age so about eight to ten years older than Mums, but it didn't seem to matter. Win was rather plump and motherly and helped in the business on the café/ballroom side of things and I was told she had a beautiful voice though I never heard her sing.

Then there was Eric and Madge. Eric was a stockbroker and looked rather like my Daddy; in fact, some people thought they were brothers but in fact they were just best friends. Eric and Madge had one son who was also called Eric, which could be a bit confusing but which seemed the thing to do then, because Reg and Win's son, Midge's brother, was also called Reg. They became known as Father Eric and Young Eric and Father Reg and Young Reg. I didn't see why they couldn't have their own names but they all seemed perfectly happy with the arrangement. Daddy had a close friend, Harold, who was unmarried; his surname was Wiggins so everyone called him Wiggy – Uncle Wiggy to me – and he was my Godfather. He wasn't very tall but he was a very good golfer. I heard he had been in love with a local girl who had married another man and he was too heartbroken to find anyone else so had stayed single.

Then there were the Clarks who had a hotel at Sandsend which consisted of several disused railway carriages which they had converted into guest rooms; they were also golfers and involved with the Am Drams, as were Mick Chapman the Accountant (who Daddy had worked with before having the hotel), and his wife, Mildred. Sam Ellison was in charge of the Customs and Excise office in the town but also in his spare time was the long-time Producer/Director of the Amateur Dramatic Society plays; he and his wife had a daughter called Bobbie who Mums was especially friendly with. Then there was the Woolleys (sorry, can't remember their Christian names) who had a son called Raymond and twin daughters, Ann and Lucy who had bright red hair and no-one, except their parents and brother Raymond could tell them apart. Raymond married Bobbie Ellison and I was their bridesmaid; I can hardly remember the wedding, but they had the reception at our hotel and it all seemed very exciting and grand.

Aunty Doff had a sister called Alice who was also in Mums' circle of friends. Alice had an admirer – well, boyfriend; he was called Philip and managed his family's clothing shop which was also on the quay, near to the licensed victualler's business where Alice and Doff lived. It was well known that they cared for each other and yet they didn't get married – I'm not sure why, but I suspect there was some objection from either Alice's Father or maybe Philip's, possibly because there was an eight year age difference between them (Alice being the older), so maybe that was it; well, who knows, but they did eventually marry after Alice's father died, but by then they were too old to have any children and it seemed crazy to me but people did have strict ideas about things like that then and handed down those sorts of prejudices. I suppose to a lesser degree it still happens.

Chapter 7

Other People

WELL, I'VE TOLD YOU about Rozzy who was a summer friend really, but my all year round school friend was Nancy. I don't really know why we were such good pals since in some ways we were quite different. Nancy's Dad worked in the bank and he and her Mum were staunch Methodists and very regular church-goers which we weren't. Even though Mums had spent time as a Sunday School teacher before marrying Daddy, their life in the hotel sort of prevented church-going and I suppose they got out of the habit in the winter too; but that didn't stop them being good people and having Christian values which in their understated way they passed on to Peter and me. Anyway, Nancy and I just 'got on' and understood each other and I somehow always knew she would be 'on my side' no matter what. I always thought of her as my best friend. Sometimes, when I was at her house I felt a bit envious of what seemed like a more normal life in a normal house, although I was perfectly all right with things at home and even in a way thought it special because of being different. I had already learned, hadn't I, that we can't have everything we want or don't want in life and can accept and adjust to the way things are?

Joy and Margo were also friends in the same form at school. Joy was very serious and sort of grown-up before she was grown-up but always fair minded and kind and Margo was sometimes slightly on another planet, dreamy and sort of 'in the clouds' and we'd jokily bring her back to earth; she loved to sing and often did, at the top of her voice when we went on one of our bike rides into the country.

When the school had singing or dancing lessons, forms 2 to 5 joined together, which was nice as we all got to know each other, in spite of the age differences. Our music teacher was Miss Crabtree who was so pretty and sweet-natured; she didn't control us very well and we took advantage of that, chattering and giggling when we ought to have been paying attention. We were a bit better behaved in the spring term when we started practicing to take part in the County Festival of Folksong, Drama and Dance which took place at the Spa over several days.

We all used to get into the spirit of the festival. It was so exciting and I loved it, especially the dancing which was either Folk or Grecian. There was singing, in choirs or individually, and we also had to perform a short play or a scene from Shakespeare and our Mums had to make our costumes. One year I got the part of Puck in *A Midsummer Night's Dream.* The Grammar School was doing the same scene and a boy called Mitch was playing Puck. I thought his costume was much better than mine and that he acted better than me, too, which was a bit annoying; but in spite of that he was the first boy I had a crush on. Anyway, in the end we came 2nd in the Drama section and the Grammar School came 4th so I can't have been so bad. It was the beginning of my interest in acting and the theatre and, I suppose, boys.

The year leading up to my eleventh birthday was an eventful one when I became more aware of the life around me, the people young and old and my place in it all. Most of it made sense, I think – we accept most things, don't we? Well, up to a point, as it's all we know; but it was during those years when I started to become more aware of what I liked or didn't and how I wanted to be and also what I didn't want, although I didn't look too far ahead or backwards. I was definitely a bit of a day-dreamer and if a lesson at school was or seemed as I've already said, well, boring, I was off into my own thoughts and missed quite a lot which I've been trying to make up for ever since. I think what I'm trying to say here is that at some point, depending on our situation and those around us, we start to form perceptions and opinions about things and people which can affect how and who we become.

On my journey to and from school and almost to the turning where I usually met Nancy and Joy there was a large garage where the mechanics would be working on cars and where, at one end, there was a display window. Sometimes there would be a new car being displayed but one day I saw a brand new racing bike on display there. I'd had a bike for a couple of years but it was an old second-hand thing, the kind we called 'a sit-up-and beg' type. I had learnt to ride on it and okay, yes, it did have wheels, but no gears and I didn't use it much; it was embarrassing, really, like an old lady's bike. The one in the window of Walker's Garage was a Raleigh and the price was £4 which was a good weekly wage for many people then. At home hardly a day passed that I didn't mention it and the fact that my birthday wasn't far away, hint, hint!

I knew I was asking a lot and there was the daily worry that one day I would pass the window and the bike would be gone and I knew there would never be another one just like it, didn't I? That bike was made for me and I knew it, dreamed about it and where it would take me and I can tell you it was a stressful time!

Well, I have to say I was pretty lucky with my parents and they had evidently given Mr Walker a deposit on the bike when I had first told them about it so that he wouldn't sell it, so I needn't have worried at all; and so it was that on the morning I became 11 years old I woke up to find that longed-for magical object of desire was no longer in Walker's window but next to my bed, all the shininess of it winking at me.

I couldn't stop looking at it – this was definitely the best day of my life so far! There it was, all sparkling new, black and silver with its pumped-up tyres, low, low handlebars and all of three gears! I felt like hugging it but instead I hugged my parents. I was I thought, after all, at that moment just about the happiest, luckiest person in the whole world.

Well as you can imagine, there was no stopping me! I was off, all around the town, and now I had the gears up and down the hills as well, no problem, sometimes standing straight up on the pedals and making it to the top then scooting down them at top speed both legs off the pedals and stuck out at the sides and sometimes no hands on the handlebars either.

Then there were the rides out to the countryside with friends at weekends or school holidays; we'd prop our bikes against a farm gate and sit on top of it for a while gazing at the cows in the field. Or it would be along the coast road to Sandsend where we'd stop and climb up onto the sea wall staring out across the ocean, wondering what lay beyond and watching the odd ship sailing by.

My bike took me to school and to visit friends and brought me home again. Sometimes it was just the two of us – we'd ride off whenever we wanted. We grew up together, my bike and I and, well, I suppose just ahead of the roller skates and tennis racquet it was my most precious possession. I'm talking about 'things' here you understand, not people, that's a different subject altogether but I needed to tell you how I will always remember that feeling of having a dream come true and how I made the most of it.

It was about this time that Daddy bought his MG sports car. He said it was more comfortable for him to drive, with his bad leg. It was second-hand but I thought it was wonderful. We named it 'Jo' because those were the letters on the number plate. I can't remember Mums riding in Jo much but I was always up for a 'spin' whenever Daddy would find time to pop off into the countryside and the lovely little villages all around Whitby, some of them right in amongst the moorlands. Looking back, these were really special times. There's something I haven't told you yet, but Daddy's name for me was 'Ubs'. Yes, I know it sounds odd! I once asked him why he called me that and he said, 'Well love, it's a derivation of that.' I said, 'What?' He said, *'Love* – it's a derivation of *love* and it's a Yorkshire word.' So that was that! I really didn't know if he made it up, you know, but I did like that it was his special name for me, and I have never ever heard the name used by or for anyone ever since. Maybe you have?

Anyway, back to Jo. I might be practising my skipping out the back, or throwing a tennis ball against a wall with my racquet when Daddy would call out, 'D'you want to come for a ride round the lanes, Ubs?' and, oh boy, did I ever! I'd leap over Jo's door without opening it. Daddy would ease himself into the driver's seat and off we'd go 'round the lanes'; sometimes it would be down Ruswarp Bank and along by the river where we might stop and watch the ducks, or it might be out towards Egton Bridge where we'd stop under the trees and Daddy would say, 'Isn't it beautiful, Ubs?' So I knew how he loved the countryside and would like to have lived there really with the birds and the wild flowers and the trees and I suppose the quietness.

Saturday mornings I had a routine. After breakfast I would go to the office and Daddy would give me five shillings, that's like 25 pence in today's money, plus I got five pence pocket money. I would then walk right down to the Yorkshire Penny Bank at the bottom of town, next to The Bridge, (well it was then) and deposit my five shillings – this was of course to teach me the importance of saving up, which I have to say has stayed with me, thank goodness. I might call in and say 'Hello' to Aunty Doff if she wasn't busy, then make my way back up the hills stopping to spend my pocket money on (1) a comic called

'School Friend', (2) a packet of stamps for my collection, and if I had any money left out of my five pence I'd get (3) a chocolate bar. Saturday afternoons in summer were on the beach as I've already said, or maybe a bike ride.

In winter with no tourists and hardly anyone else around, loads of us would meet up at the top of the Prom (the Promenade, but usually called 'The Cliff') and roller skate all the way down to the bottom which is more than half a mile and where there's a statue of Captain Cook. We were a mix of kids from all the schools; some I knew and some I didn't, but it was good fun. I envied the ones, mostly the boys, who could go all the way down the cliff crouching down in what we called 'little man' which meant in a sitting-down position clutching the front of your shoes; whenever I tried to do it I fell over backwards which was so annoying and embarrassing because the boys used to laugh and call out 'Ha ha, she's bum-heavy!' which puzzled me, not why they called me that, but as to why I couldn't do 'Little Man' because I was quite skinny. Mums used to say I didn't eat enough to keep a bird alive and it's true – I really wasn't all that interested in food; anyway, I eventually gave up on 'little man' and got quite good at doing circles and turns. In the nineteen-thirties roller skates, ours anyway, had to be clipped onto your shoes, so you had to have fairly heavy shoes and there was a key to tighten the clips so they stayed on – well, you hoped they did! If they fell off you could go a right tumble.

In winter, way back then, Sundays were very quiet when all the shops were shut. They were shut on Sundays in the summertime too, but being a seaside holiday town there was still plenty going on and lots of people about then.

Sundays in winter really were very, very quiet. Depending on the weather it would be golfing for Daddy and Mums and I expect I would begrudgingly do my homework among other things. There were some programmes on the radio I would listen to but I couldn't sit still for long – I might practice my dancing in the dining room or read a book. Compared to all the technical things children have these days, we had to think of things to occupy ourselves. Afternoons, Daddy and I often went for a walk round the outskirts of town so I got to know my way around pretty well. He had a walking stick and I asked if I could have one too so one day we walked down town to Blenkey's Tobacconists where he bought a small size one for me, I felt so important and grown up.

Christmas was in some ways quite different then, to how it is now. I suppose that we, and of course the traders have followed the American tradition of much gift-giving, decoration, fairy lights, a real tree and turkey for the Christmas meal. In the hotel, which of course was mainly closed up, we had an imitation tree which stood in the hall on the porter's desk so we only saw it if we went in or out that way and we didn't put our presents under it as we do now for all to see; anyway, as I didn't have any money I didn't buy presents and mine were delivered by Father Christmas (of course) late on Christmas Eve, put in a pillow case hung at the end of my bed. I used to be so excited I had trouble going to sleep and one night I heard the presents being delivered and no, I definitely did not peep to see if it really was Santa Claus, I just pretended to be asleep, of course! Up until the time Peter went away to boarding school we had shared a room and it was fun opening our presents together, but then I was on my own; I didn't mind really, it was the way it was and I would soon be off waking everybody up to show them what I had.

I usually had a party sometime in December, inviting all my school friends. We had it in the big hotel lounge with the fire on and Daddy was in charge of his prized radiogram, playing music for Pass the Parcel or Musical Chairs. As we got older we played 'Sardines' or 'Murder' and it was usually potted meat sandwiches, jelly and ice cream at the end with crackers and a fun present to take home. I got invited to their parties as well and there would be sometimes seven or eight during December, some on the same day, so you had to choose which one to go to which was hard.

The only decoration we had in our little living room were sprigs of Holly and Christmas cards propped up on the mantelpiece; arranging them artistically around the walls, elaborate decorations and fairy lights didn't seem to have occurred to people then. There were two Dances that Mums and Daddy and their friends always went to around Christmas time – one was the Golf Dance and the other was the Hospital Ball; they were both held at James' Ballroom which was the one owned by Reg and Win, our family friends. I used to love seeing my parents getting all dressed up to go and enjoyed the excitement of it all, but apart from that, nothing else much happened at Christmas: a bit more visiting by friends and delivering presents, perhaps, and although it seems more celebrated now, Christmas did feel special and I look back on it as a wonderful time.

I want to tell you about Holly and Basil. They were two gentlemen who owned and ran a hotel of similar size to ours and about 200 yards further up the cliff at the other side of the tennis court area. Daddy and Mums liked them a lot but didn't really get to meet up with them very much because, like ours and all the other hotels, theirs closed in the winter and they went off to London where they had another home and Basil worked in the theatre. Holly was older and I suppose, retired; I thought they were related in some way, like brothers or uncle and nephew, but somehow I eventually understood that they were what is now called a gay partnership. I used to love to catch site of them when they would walk past Princess Royal after a trip down town; well, they sort of strolled slowly, elegantly and were dressed very theatrically and Basil usually had a large bunch of flowers on his arm. Holly often wore a camel hair coat and they just seemed so glamorous and interesting to me and I thought how I would have loved to talk to them about their life in London. I know that some of the guests who came to stay at Holly and Basil's hotel were theatre people from London; one in particular Bets and I used to see sometimes on her way to the Spa in the early evening: we didn't know her name but we christened her 'Pink Shrimp' – I suppose that was because she was always dressed in some elaborate pink concoction and was a tiny lady. She wore very high heeled shoes and we took her age to be, well, rather old, so she did totter rather than walk down the cliff to her evenings on the Spa and we loved to catch site of her.

It was that same year I was 11 that a new boy called Michael came to our school. He would only be 10 because, as you already know, boys left when they were 10 or 11. Anyway it happened that he had just moved to Whitby with his mother and older sister to live with an aunt who lived in the Crescent opposite to our hotel, so we would walk back and forth to school together each day and became friends. We arranged to meet each day at the corner where the Crescent turned in to Crescent Avenue but Michael was hardly ever there, so I would go to their house to call for him. They were a jokey lot in their house, especially his mum who was a large lady with a smiley face who used to tease me and make jokes which I didn't understand but would join in the laughter anyway trying not to seem dumb. They were somehow different from my parents' friends but interesting and I liked the times I spent there. One day Michael and I made a pact that when we went to bed one night we would talk to each other across the Crescent from each other's dormer bedroom windows which were both in the roof spaces; of course we had to shout and we only did it once, for it was a bit embarrassing as people walking along below would look up and point at us, not surprising really. My parents were out, on the Spa probably, so they never knew we did that, thank goodness. Michael had to leave the following year to go to the Grammar School so I didn't see him much after that but it was nice to have him as a neighbour and to have a friend who was a boy.

By the time I was 13 years old, I was well used to my life in the different Summer/Winter routines. The excitement of early Spring and the hustle and bustle of the hotel opening up, Chef and Flo and the rest returning, lovely, bossy but kind Flo who kept asking me if I wanted a chocolate biscuit or a banana which she knew I always did and the delights of the Spa, the beach, the tennis courts, well, just everything coming to life again. Not that the winter days were dull, anything but, just quieter and different.

It wasn't long after my thirteenth birthday that my periods started. I knew it was going to happen because it had already happened to my school friend Joy, (she who was grown up before she was grown up!) and so, of course, she had told the rest of us. Anyway there was also my closeness to cousin Bets and her friend Midge who were three years older than me and informants to me about all sorts of things. I wasn't happy about it at all, but knew it had to be – there was no escaping it; it didn't really seem to help to be told it was a sign you were growing up. I didn't feel ready for that, for I liked my life as it was and I wanted to stay being a kid. I suppose nature had different ideas, though, as I was beginning to be a bit interested in boys and was aware they seemed interested in me, and as I learned later in life, nothing stays the same and anyway that was the year that life was about to change dramatically for all of us. The year was 1939.

Chapter 8

War

THAT YEAR, the one leading up to the start of World War 2 and the one when I became a teenager, although we weren't called that then, was pretty strange. In one way we thought the war wasn't going to happen because the Prime Minister at that time, Neville Chamberlain, had apparently had a meeting the year before in Germany with Adolph Hitler and agreed to sign a Peace Treaty. Of course we eventually found out that Hitler never intended to keep that agreement and the Government, being suspicious, had begun making defensive preparations and other plans in case the worst was to happen.

That summer of 1939 was mostly like all the others, for me anyway. I had my season ticket for the Spa, Frank Gomez still led the Orchestra, and Roz and I would roam around there in the evenings. There was still dancing to a live band after the shows in the theatre which we would watch from the gallery above. There were still days at the hut on the beach and bike rides with Nancy or Margo; but there was also a strange feeling of unease as we would hear the adults discussing what was happening across the Channel and I can remember my Uncle Bert once saying in a very serious voice, 'It's happening again, and this time it's to our children.'

At the time he said that we were all on the beach munching our sandwiches and we stopped chewing and looked at each other as his words sunk in and I think in that moment we realised how serious and maybe how close the possibility of a war was, and we couldn't pretend it wasn't happening any longer. My Brother Peter was 17 years old, Harry my cousin was 18, Bets and Midge were 16, so all were in line to be conscripted into the armed forces as soon, or soon after a war began. So although our summer holiday fun continued as usual there was this air of uncertainty and, I suppose fear, hanging over us. The hotel was doing well and had built up a good reputation, offering well-appointed, well run, comfortable accommodation close to the sea; there was also the Spa and sports ground and the Chef's Cordon Bleu food, finally Daddy and Mums were getting some benefit from their hard work, worries and investment. Then it happened: after the hustle and bustle of August and some worrying news from London, it was on the 3rd of September that we gathered round the wireless in our little sitting room, Chef, Flo and the rest of our staff leaning in at the door to hear the announcement from the Prime Minister that Hitler had broken the agreement of the so-called Peace Treaty and had invaded Poland and therefore we were now at war with Germany.

Well, you can imagine how shattered and in shock we all felt, although it had been sort of expected. Now it was real and no-one really knew what to expect or what to do. The guests were all buzzing and gathered together in groups and saying they would have to leave and queueing up at the office window asking Daddy for their bills. Poor Daddy in the trauma of the occasion could hardly insist they pay for the time left of their stay which meant a big loss on his projected revenue. And of course the phone started ringing and ringing with bookings for September being cancelled, as all holidays like most plans were now being called off for the foreseeable future.

That night was very strange. All the guests had departed, the daily staff too had gone home to their families earlier than usual and only Chef, Flo and the resident staff remained, but they too were packing up, about to collect their final wages and go back to Leeds, Middlesbrough or wherever. No-one knew what to expect, least of all me and others my age. I suppose we were just waiting to be told what to do, or what we couldn't do.

For some reason that night, Mums, Daddy and I moved from our top floor Summer bedroom down the stairs to sleep in one of the larger first floor guest rooms. It had a double and a single bed in it. Peter was still at home so I expect he moved down as well but I don't remember that. I do know Daddy told him he would have to leave his boarding school after the next term as our financial situation had changed now. Peter said, 'That's fine because I'm joining the forces as soon as I can.' We all knew that was what most young men would be thinking, one way or another, but I didn't like the look on Daddy's face – the whole thing was tearing him apart. I went to bed before Mums and Daddy but I couldn't sleep and later when they came up I heard Mums crying and Daddy trying to comfort her; it was horrible and sad and yet nice all at the same time and I knew our lives and everyone else's had changed. I don't remember there being any panic, just a reluctant acceptance of the situation and everyone doing what they felt they had to do, exchanging sympathies and understandings and having the wireless on all the time to hear any important announcements. I suppose the Government, the Armed Forces chiefs and the Intelligence lot were all busy working out what had to be done to counteract the expected German attacks whatever form they would take and that was brought home to us when about three days after the announcement that we were at war, two Army Officers walked into our hotel and declared it was to be requisitioned, taken over for their use for the duration of the war. I think you can probably guess how my parents felt, suddenly faced with losing home and business with little or no time to plan what to do or where to go.

The first regiment to move in within days was the Royal Signals and the hotel became their Officers' Mess. Although they could requisition the building, the order didn't apply to the furnishings, but as they needed them at that time, they negotiated with Daddy to pay him a rental, I think it was 5 pounds a week to keep all the furniture in place. However, as the war progressed regiments moved out and others moved in and used the property in whatever way was needed, sometimes as offices when they would move the furniture up to the top floor or once, as Brigade Headquarters, when they probably hauled some of it out again. Daddy didn't have any say in what happened but he and Mums were allowed to have a bedroom and what had been Chef and Flo's room as a kitchen. Daddy rented a house nearby for Aunt Alice, me and Peter, until he could sort something else out for us, which in the end didn't happen, but I'll tell you about that later.

Most of the hotels and Bed and Breakfast places in the town were occupied by the troops either in training or waiting deployment to the front lines of action or defence; Whitby in effect became a garrison town. At one time a Tank Regiment regularly used the moorlands for training their personnel and Gun Crews were posted on the cliff. Barbed wire was quickly erected along the whole length of the Promenade and cliff top. We were all soon issued with gas masks which we were told to carry with us everywhere we went, and also ration books as most food especially that imported from abroad would soon be in short supply – and definitely there would be no more bananas for me!

We all soon knew the sound of an air-raid warning, a screaming siren rising up then down; the all-clear was when the high-pitched sound was a level tone. Everyone had to make sure that all their windows were blacked out and no lights shone through at night as even any slight chink of light could attract enemy aircraft. None of the street lights were turned on at night so we became used to depending on the moon and cloudless nights to see our way as although torches were allowed, they had only to be used in emergencies and then kept face down and not flashed about. The air-raid warnings were fairly frequent, almost straight away, because the Germans wanted to target our industrial towns, especially those with ports and shipping like Newcastle and Middlesbrough so their flight path would inevitably be over or close to Whitby, which lies to the south on the same coastline. Men and women who were either too young or too old to join the forces could join the defensive Home Guard, become Air-raid wardens, or man the 24-hour communications and coastguard stations which were quickly re-organised.

Peter went back to his school for one last term and took his exams before he left at Christmas and enlisted when he was 17 and a half the following February. He joined the RAF and hoped to be trained to fly but was rejected because of his poor eyesight, so he had to settle for ground crew; we knew that he was sent to a base overseas but we weren't allowed to know where and although we had an occasional censored letter we didn't see him again for the rest of the war.

I went back to school as usual for the winter term and one quite good thing was that although Uncle Bert went back to London the rest of the family stayed at Havelock Place and Bets went to my school, for the next few terms. Harry joined the Army and became a Commando and we eventually found out that his unit had been sent to defend Crete but that they were taken prisoner there and he spent the rest of the war in a German prisoner of war camp. Harry tried to escape twice but failed and when he finally came home, it was a long time before he could stop obsessively washing his hands and he just wasn't the same happy-go-lucky Harry anymore.

Christmas that year-end was very low key as you can imagine, and there was also some severe weather, very cold and lots of snow. Those of us who had toboggans hauled them to the nearest steep hill and made the most of it and even found a frozen pond to skate on, though it was more falling about than skating as I remember.

In the February of 1940 when Peter left to join the RAF, Daddy gave up renting the house and managed to arrange for Aunt Alice and I to move back into the hotel, but soon after that there was a rumour going around that the Germans were planning to invade us and that one of their target areas was our North East coast. Caithy called a meeting for parents to ask them if they would agree to the school evacuating to somewhere safer. It was a big decision but the majority voted in favour so it was then up to us kids to say whether we wanted to be evacuated or stay behind and go to another school. In the end, all the senior girls chose to stay behind which left my form and group of friends the oldest of those who chose to go. I didn't want to leave my parents, but it was all happening so fast and I suppose in one way it seemed like a bit of an adventure and as my closest friends were going too it felt okay, like we were all in the same boat.

So, it was all arranged in a hurry and seemed no time at all before Nancy, Margo, Joy, me and the rest of us were boarding a bus to set off across the country to Ambleside in the Lake District which is a tourist area to the west of Yorkshire with no heavy industry so much less chance of it being bombed. We just didn't like to think about the suspected invasion. Apart from our own clothes and things, we had to take our own bed and bedding which went ahead in a removal van. Apart from the teachers, Caithy, Gogs, Bowlegs, Miss Crabtree (music) and Miss Wheeler (maths) there was a cook and one other domestic helper who had travelled earlier to get the house ready.

We were all excited to see where we were going to be and what it would be like. Apart from the odd day trip to Scarborough, I hadn't been anywhere but Whitby before. Eventually, we reached Windermere and the lake which is the largest one in the Lake District; it was very beautiful and Gogs announced that we would soon be at Ambleside. At long last the bus turned into a narrow lane and drove up a steep hill and then into a driveway between bushes and trees until we came to a fairly large Victorian house with a porch at the front and we all tumbled out and were told to collect our cases and go inside and for the older ones to look after the younger ones. We were soon told where our bedrooms were and Joy, Nancy, Margo and I were all together as well as Maureen, who although she was a couple of years younger than us was in our form because she was so clever for her age.

It was all a bit muddly that first day, but we unpacked and made up our beds before someone rang a bell to get us all downstairs for tea. Gogs talked about how things were going to be, or, more to the point, not be. Some of the younger ones were showing signs of missing home and their Mums and Dads, so we were asked to help see them into bed, talk to them and read them stories. Then it was bedtime for us as well. We all felt pretty strange and talked about it all, then whispered until it was lights out and 'no more talking girls'. Before I fell asleep I wondered whether I had made the right decision to go away with the school, away from home, except it wasn't really home anymore, was it? – It was, yet it wasn't. It was full of the army and my parents didn't have any control over what happened to it anymore, but there was no protesting about anything then: everything was about what could be done to help the war effort.

Anyway, I had agreed to go and I was stuck with it. I suppose in a way it was a help to have me out of the muddle at home and safer, but as I fell asleep I really didn't know what to think and I expect my friends felt the same way.

The school house in Ambleside was called Broadings and was, as I said, halfway up one of the hillsides that surround the town. From our bedroom window we had a view over the lake and countryside and the house was bordered by several acres of woodland which we were soon exploring. The day we had arrived was a Friday so we had the weekend to settle in and get into some sort of routine. On Sunday we were escorted by one of the teachers to Ambleside church, well, if you were C of E, that is; the Methodists, Joy, Nancy and a few others, were taken to that Church. There were no Catholics as it happened.

 The trips to church soon became the highlight of our week, not least because Maureen and I got a massive crush on one of the choir boys and, would you believe it, used sign language to try to get him and his friends to come up the hill to meet us! We did this during prayer times when whoever was in charge of us had her head bowed. This was massively risky as in those days, any communication between boys and girls of our age was strictly limited, and especially as we were in the care of our school teachers who were obviously aware of how responsible they were for us. But we were young teenagers and missing the freedom we had enjoyed at home so we were only looking for a bit of excitement to brighten up what was a pretty boring time and our motives couldn't have been more innocent. Believe it or not, the boys did understand our dodgy hand signals and eventually did come up the hill and we met them in the woods; we sat round in a circle on a patch of grass chatting and giggling happily, when suddenly lo and behold, Caithy appeared walking towards us on the path from the school looking very grim, which is putting it mildly! The staff must have guessed we were up to something. Anyway, after a severe talking to, the boys were shooed away never to darken our woods again and we were summoned to Caithy's study for another severe talking to. Although it was something that would be considered quite natural today, and even then it was harmless fun, I thought we were made to feel more wicked and ashamed than we really deserved. Oh well, I suppose we had broken the rules and caused worry for those in charge who must have thought we were less innocent than we were and feared the worst.

A lot of the time at Ambleside was helping with the younger children because my form mates and I were the oldest ones and the school was now in a boarding situation which involved a lot more supervision time than in a day school. I didn't mind that at all, but as time went on I became aware of the fact that our study times did seem to be affected. Don't get me wrong, I wasn't by any means the studious type, but my friends felt the same in that we weren't somehow learning a lot and we knew we should be preparing for our School Leaving Exam (the School Cert) which we were due to sit in two years' time. We did a lot of singing, especially (for some reason) 'Waltzing Matilda', the Australian song, and reading poetry, which I enjoyed; but I did really miss my dancing lessons, netball and gym. We had to be content with going for long walks which was fine because the area was so pretty and interesting and we would pick wild flowers and then press them in our exercise books. In the autumn we formed our own Girl Scout Troop and started earning badges, but as the days shortened I began to feel more and more homesick and depressed, wondering how Mums and Daddy were getting on and where on earth Peter was and what was going to happen to all of us.

We wrote letters home every week and had letters from our parents, but I knew they wouldn't tell me if things were difficult or worrying. Daddy had volunteered to re-join the RAF but of course he didn't pass the medical exam, even to be ground staff so he had to be content with just watching his home and business being used in the war effort, well, more like it being wrecked. He wrote that he was earning some money by returning to his Accountancy skills and doing the books for local businesses. Mums was helping out at the communications office. One day, two of the younger children at school, Sheila and John, a sister and brother, were called out of class to Caithys' office to be told that their father had been killed; he was in the Navy and his convoy had been torpedoed crossing the Atlantic. We all felt so helpless and sad, it brought the war closer. Joy's father was in the regular Merchant Navy as many Whitby men were, and he too was later killed when his ship was destroyed. Joy was so brave and told us she had been half expecting it. A few years earlier when Joy was ten years old, she had been on one of her father's lengthy voyages which it was hoped would help to clear up a serious chest problem she had; unfortunately it didn't, but she did have a whole term off school and we were all very envious. I think that she must have felt so glad to have had that special time with her father and secretly even though it felt selfish and somehow wrong, I was glad that my Father wasn't able to be in the front line.

Christmas came and went and there was a lot of snow which was fun for a while. The lake froze over and the hills around looked beautiful, but as Spring approached and my 15th birthday in May, I began to plead with my parents when I wrote to let me come home. They had told me in their letters that dear Aunt Alice had gone into a nursing home. I'm sure the drastic changes the war had brought had affected her – she must have felt so disorientated and deprived of her normal routine; but strangely perhaps, it made me want to be part of what was going on there and not to be protected from it. I just really wanted to be back in Whitby

We knew the war wasn't going very well for us. The big attempt to stop Hitler in his tracks with the Normandy landings had failed, Winston Churchill had taken over as Prime Minister and was proving to be a strong leader, encouraging and giving hope and resolve and there was now a coalition government of both major political parties. London and other major cities were being relentlessly bombarded and everything, but everything was geared towards us winning the war: the alternative was too horrible to think about and beside that we didn't yet know about the dreadful things happening to the Jewish people in Germany.

At what would have been the Easter break Daddy came for me in Jo. I was so happy but it was hard saying goodbye to those I had become close to, those my age and some of the young ones as well; we had become a family in many ways and I knew I would miss their company and friendship. Also, there had been good times, walking the hills and riding our bikes in the lovely Lakeland countryside; but I felt sure it was time for me to leave, and of course my trusty, beloved bike had to go with me and somehow got squeezed into Jo as well. I don't remember how or when my bed, etc., made the journey back, but I suppose my parents arranged that somehow or maybe they just left it there.

Not long after my departure from Broadings, Nancy and Margo also left. Nancy went to a Quaker boarding school, Margo to a small local private one and later I heard that Hildathorpe had closed down altogether so Joy and Maureen and the rest had to return to Whitby as well. I think the worry and maybe the financial side of running a boarding facility during the war had become too difficult for Caithy and Gogs who I heard had eventually sold Broadings and retired from teaching, but had stayed in the Lake District.

Chapter 9

Another School – Same War

IT WAS SO GOOD to be home, although of course, as I keep saying, it wasn't home any more – well, it was and yet it wasn't. Although the building belonged to us, we had no say in what happened there and were only allowed in the rooms allocated to us, namely the small living room and two first floor bedrooms plus the makeshift kitchen and a bathroom. Mums had made Aunt Alice's room ready for me and it became my refuge; the rest of the building was full of soldiers – it was still being used as an Officers' Mess but a different lot to the ones who were there before I went to Ambleside. I soon got used to it and would exchange 'hello's' if I saw them, but mostly we kept ourselves to ourselves; it was all very serious and everyone, civilians or service people, young and old, just adapted to the new situations as they happened.

I went to see Aunt Alice in the nursing home and she seemed to be okay in her sweet accepting sort of way. I think she thought it was just a temporary arrangement, as I suppose we had all hoped. Betty and Midge had both joined the W.A.A.F. (the Women's Air Force). Aunt Nan and Audrey had gone back to London to be with Uncle Bert and Havelock Place was full of soldiers billeted there with dear little Aunt Sally coping as best as she could. Audrey had volunteered to work for the Ambulance Service in London which was worthy stuff with all the bombing going on there.

The big question, for me anyway, was where I was to finish my education. My parents had been asking around for any alternatives to the Grammar School which I had told them for some reason I was dead against, scared probably, but it couldn't have been any worse than where I did end up. There was, or had been a convent boarding school on the edge of town called St Marys and like Hildathorpe, they had evacuated although not like us to the Lake District, but much further, to Canada. However some of the teaching nuns who had stayed behind with the Mother Superior had carried on as a small day school for those children left behind and who, like me, didn't fancy the Grammar, so that's where I went.

It was my first taste of being in a totally different school environment. There were so few pupils, about twelve in all so that we all shared one classroom. The Mother Superior, who we had to call 'Mother', taught History and she was okay but had a really boring voice and I struggled to stay awake in her lessons. If your marks weren't good enough you would have to go to her office, which was called 'Long Suffering' (?!) to be lectured to, but I could hardly tell her that her boring voice was my main problem, could I? And then, just like it had been at Broadings, there were no arrangements for sport or gym and I missed that. I still liked and did fairly well in English, French and Art, and hoped I would gain my school leaving certificate with those subjects plus hopefully Botany and R.E. which is, after two rather difficult years, what happened.

The main difficulty there was that there were two pupils, Amy and June, already there who at the makeshift school that St Mary's had temporarily become, acted like self-appointed wardens for the rest of us and unfortunately seemed to enjoy getting us into trouble with the staff. Perhaps they had been asked to keep an eye on things as initially they would have been the oldest ones, but then I arrived and came from a school where we looked after each other and, well, it was just completely not what I was used to and, I have to admit, I didn't know how to handle it. I tried making friends with them but that didn't seem to work. The older one, Amy, was the leader of this strange little gang of two but June, two years younger, was a willing accomplice.

One day one of the younger nuns, Sister Patience, said she wished to speak to me privately which filled me with dread at what I might be going to be accused of doing, or not doing. She took me for a walk in the school grounds during which she completely shocked me by saying she was very concerned about me as 'it had come to her attention' that I was 'consorting' with the soldiers in my 'place of residence' which she didn't consider was a safe place for me to be living and also that it meant I was a bad influence on the rest of the school! I was so taken aback that someone who didn't know me, my parents or the situation, would assume or believe such a thing, and I couldn't help wondering who could have 'brought to her attention' this totally wrong view of me and my situation at home.

I was fifteen and, compared to most fifteen year olds of today, I was sexually very innocent. I worried about the war, my family, our changed circumstances, and was only just starting to be vaguely interested in my body and in boys my own age. I guessed what she meant by the word 'consorting' and I knew it meant more than, well, talking. It actually hadn't occurred to me though that I was in any danger at home, quite the opposite in fact – the truth was that I felt very well protected! Obviously I tried to explain how things really were to Sister Patience but she seemed to have made up her mind about me and I felt angry and somehow helpless to have been so misjudged. Anyway, soon after this I did discover that it had indeed been Amy and June who had given the nuns such a completely wrong view of me and my life at home and I found it hard to come to terms with.

I couldn't bring myself to tell my parents. I knew it would have horrified them so I kept it to myself, which didn't really help me deal with it or the misplaced shame of it. I think the staff eventually realised they could have been wrong to so quickly believe what was basically malicious gossip and may even have become aware of how unkind the two girls could be, although there wasn't any apology and I didn't ever confront them about the subject. I just wanted to forget it and the apparent need to give me a 'bad name' or maybe get rid of me, who knows, I didn't understand any of it or them.

I welcomed the summer holidays even though the news from the war zones wasn't good and so much was different from previous summers. The rumoured invasion of our coast hadn't happened and everyone seemed to have adjusted to all the restrictions and to be coping with the fact that our town was teeming with soldiers and army vehicles and stuff. Daddy had had to sell a terrace of houses in York which he had been hoping to keep for their retirement fund; he told me they sold for £200 each, yet were evidently large four-storey Victorian houses. Of course, with all the bombing, property was worth very little but Daddy, being deprived of his business, needed to draw in whatever money he could.

Mums was obviously just as worried about the situation and one day told me she had answered an advertisement for a job in London to manage a block of service flats. I didn't like the idea of her going away, but with things the way they were I didn't feel it would be right to complain or try to stop her. I expect Daddy felt the same but he didn't say and I suppose I didn't like to ask. Whatever we were all feeling it wasn't going to change things and we all just had to deal with it. It had been quickly accepted generally in the whole country that whatever happened, you didn't complain; everyone's priority was helping to win the war and to defeat Adolph Hitler, his German Nazi Party and to prevent their goal of world domination.

I used to pop into the nursing home to see Aunt Alice every now and then and she always seemed pleased to see me, bless her, and seemed her usual accepting un-complaining self; however, she evidently wasn't well at all and in August her condition deteriorated and she passed away quietly and without fuss as she had lived. I really felt so sad, that dear sweet little lady, sister to my Grandma Nell, had been so close to us and part of our lives for so long and yet I realised I hardly knew her. I didn't have any idea how old she was or what she thought about anything. The night she died I cried into my pillow feeling an emptiness and loss I didn't fully understand.

So September of 1941 arrived and I had to return to St Marys' where I felt so alien and friendless; however, Maureen was there now, having returned from Broadings so at least I had an ally, but she was put through the same things such as sometimes the two hostile girls not speaking to her all day, or worse, being whispered about. Then they told the nuns that she smoked, which she did but only in secret at home, so why tell? Well, at least Maureen and I had each other now and could talk to each other about it, but what I eventually realised to be a type of bullying didn't really help us during that difficult time or with our studying.

It was strange the way the younger children were controlled into thinking it was all just a game and went along with all the sniggering and silent treatment and also that the nuns didn't seem to notice what was going on and why on earth didn't Maureen and I tell them? I can't answer that except that maybe it was because we were in unfamiliar territory with no knowledge of classmates who were alien and told lies about us to the staff It was my first experience of having to be with people who were not, like my dear friend Nancy, 'always on my side'.

Mums got the job in London which was really brave of her, with all the bombing there. She wrote to Daddy and me every week and telephoned sometimes. I missed her so much but Daddy and I managed okay. Some nights we'd play cards, a game he taught me, called Bezique, or we'd go to the cinema at the weekend, if I'd done my homework. Daddy's friend Eric would call for him once or twice a week to go to their Men's Club for a game of snooker and a beer or two and sometimes one of the Officers would come through from the front part of the building to our little room for a chat, usually about the war and I'd make them a cup of tea.

I know Daddy was missing Mums but he didn't complain, and I think just wanted to keep me as happy and safe as he could and our financial 'heads above water'. It was a strange situation in a way but didn't really seem so at the time; everyone was doing what they could to cope or survive and most families were separated one way or another.

December came and as the Christmas holidays approached and Maureen and I had coped with another term at St Marys, something happened to change the course of the war. It was on the 7th December that news came through to us that Japanese planes had bombed Pearl Harbour at Hawaii where the American Navy kept some of their fleet. Until that happened the United States had stayed away from getting involved in the European struggle, apart that is from selling us, by a lease/lend arrangement, some badly-needed military and other equipment; so for the first two years (1939 – 1941) the British Isles had been alone in keeping Nazi Germany at bay and in providing a haven for those who managed to escape from Europe such as General De Gaulle who had formed the Free French Army as well as Polish, Dutch and Belgian, the Scandinavians and many from our Colonies who individually joined up with our forces. As Italy under the dictator Mussolini had joined with Germany it had also become our enemy.

However, the United States were now involved in the war totally as our allies and against all the aggression. It has been well recorded that Hitler with his well-armed, well-trained German forces then made a bad decision in attacking Russia rather than what he considered to be an easy target, Britain. What his well trained troops were not prepared for though was an extremely severe Russian winter so that the Germans suffered huge damages and loss of life causing them to retreat very much the worse for the experience and by then much less inclined or equipped to come across the English Channel.

That year Christmas was naturally very different. So strange without Mums and it must have been awful for her on her own in war ravaged London. Anyway, Daddy took me to both the Hospital and Golf Christmas Balls which were held as usual in James' Ballroom, the money raised going to the war effort. I didn't have a dress or enough coupons or money to buy one so Daddy and I searched through Mums clothes to find something we could adapt to fit me. Daddy was okay – he'd had the same Dinner Suit since he was a young man and always looked great. I was so excited to be going at last although of course as much as I loved Daddy to bits, I would have liked to have been going with someone my own age or with a group of young people, but none of my friends were around now and my only school friend at the moment, Maureen, was too young as she was three years younger than me, although as I've said she already smoked cigarettes! It just never appealed to me – I just couldn't see the sense of it, sort of sucking smoke into your body and though friends, including Mo, kept telling me it was a good feeling and I ought to try it, I just didn't want to. Well now we all know how damaging to health tobacco is so I'm glad I felt as I did and am really angry that cigarettes were promoted so much back then and even encouraged as being calming to the nerves and a relief from stress which of course everyone was needing; but there was no mention of the harmful effect to heart and lungs, etc., or how hard it is to stop once you start.

The dances were okay. I safety-pinned Mums' dress to fit into my waist and felt reasonably glamorous and enjoyed the experience. We sat at a table with my parents' friends, the ones I've told you about and I danced with the 'uncles' and with Daddy as well even though his leg stopped us whirling around the floor as I loved to do. The only young people there were the few lucky enough to be home on leave or those stationed in the town. At the Golf Dance, one young man in army uniform did come over and ask me for a dance which I thought was quite brave of him with Daddy and all my 'uncles and aunts' sitting around me, so that was nice and we chatted a bit; his name was Charlie and he asked if we could meet up and go for a walk the next day which we did, all the way to the village of Newholm, about two miles along a narrow country lane, holding hands with the frost on the trees and biting at our noses. It turned out that Charlie was a local lad; he told me his regiment were soon to be sent abroad but of course he couldn't say where. When we said 'Goodbye' we had a cuddle and he kissed me and it was lovely – it was my first real 'date' and I knew I liked him. Anyway it was only a few weeks later that I learnt he had been killed. I was heartbroken.

Chapter 10

Sweet Sixteen and Somewhere over the Rainbow

DADDY AND I saw the New Year of 1942 in at his friends Eric and Madge's house. Their son who as you know was also called Eric was home on leave from the Navy; he was six years older than me but we were good friends and put some music on and showed our parents how to Jive – we had picked it up from seeing American films. Soon after that Daddy persuaded Mums to give up the job in London and come back, which she eventually did after she had given a month's notice. In the meantime I was back at school coping as best as I could and Daddy and I muddled along helping each other to manage in our army barracks situation. I never told him about the problem at school; after all, I had chosen to go there instead of the Grammar School, hadn't I? so, it was a question of sticking it out; after all, I only had another year of it and Mums arrived back just before my sixteenth birthday in May.

I was getting interested in fashion and how I looked, perhaps due to seeing American films and the weekly Women's magazine which I now bought with my pocket money instead of a comic. It was all in my head though, as we had so little money and we were also restricted by the clothes coupons we were issued which had to be used for essentials like school uniforms, shoes and if possible a warm winter coat or raincoat. There were only two dress shops in Whitby then and the most fashionable one was owned by my fiend Maureen's Mum, so of course she was in a good position to have more or less what she wanted of which I have to admit being a bit, okay, a lot, jealous. I mean, that's the way it was: if your father was a butcher then obviously your family were not going to go short of sausages, and if you were a scrap metal dealer you would most likely get rich. The war caused all kinds of mix-ups but on the whole those who had access to certain things shared with those who hadn't – there was a general feeling of wanting to help one another.

Mums started to work at the Council Offices which was where the local defence system was co-ordinated and she had become friendly with the wife of the new local railway Station Master. She was from Russia and had been a member of the Bolshoi Ballet. I'm telling you this because this lady who was called Irina and who was visiting us one day, asked me if I liked to dance. Well, as you can imagine I told her how much I loved dancing and that I missed the classes we had at my school before the war but that I had never studied any Ballet, only Greek, Scottish (reels) and Ballroom. Irina then asked if I would like to have some tuition from her as I was 'nicely turned out' (she meant my feet were turned out which is important for ballet) and I jumped up and said, 'Would I ever! Yes please!' – and that was how I fell in love with ballet, only unfortunately a few years too late to be serious about it. Anyway, I loved my private lessons and I'm sure the time I spent with Irina helped me in certain ways through my life, improved posture, muscle tone and the discipline of practising for two hours every day. For a while I did feel desperate to have a career in some form of dance but the timing just wasn't right, was it? It seemed to be far too frivolous a thing to be thinking about doing when we were in the middle of a World War. Anyway the dance sessions also helped me a lot to counteract the stupid situation at school as I was trying to study for the end of school exams, the School Certificate. Daddy tried his best to help me with Maths but I guess I just wasn't a 'numbers' person, not then anyway. I think I already knew I was a 'words' person and I had my parents and dear old Goggs to thank for that.

A girl called Joan who had been in the form above me at Hildathorpe and who had sort of taken me under her wing a few years earlier when she told me about 'the facts of life,' called on me one day and asked if I'd like to go for a bike ride to Sandsend. When Hildathorpe had evacuated to Ambleside Joan had opted to go to the Grammar School so I hadn't seen her for some time – so I was quite surprised really but pleased that she would think of me and it was a lovely June day, so off we went. It's about three miles to Sandsend, past the golf lincs and the sea rolling in, and as we rode through the village where the sands actually do end and where the cliffs curve round forming a bay, Joan said, 'We'll stay here for a while before we go back.'

'Okay,' I said.

We skidded to a stop where a boy was leaning on his bike by the sea wall and Joan obviously knew him from the Grammar School; anyway, she introduced me to him and I couldn't help thinking how good-looking he was: he had dark curly hair and very blue eyes which were staring at me rather a lot, I thought. He was called Paul and after we'd chatted a bit he cycled half way along the road back to Whitby with us, then he stopped and called out 'See you again sometime!' and went back to Sandsend where he lived.

Needless to say, on our way home I asked Joan about Paul and she then told me that one day at school he had asked her to arrange for us to meet, so the bike ride had all been a set up! Don't ask me where or when he had seen me, but Whitby's a small town and I had mixed with a lot of girls and boys from the Grammar School, roller skating, Christmas parties, down town on Saturdays, in fact I don't really know why I hadn't chosen to go to the Grammar but, well, there you are, I hadn't and we all make mistakes, especially when we don't know what's ahead. The next day, believe it or not, there was a phone call for me from Paul asking me out and, yes, I did say 'yes' because, wouldn't you know, I was so happy! It seemed like I actually had a boyfriend, someone who seemed to like me and all of a sudden, the war, the girls at school, situation at home, no future as a dancer or us being poor, none of it mattered any more, I was like Dorothy in the Wizard of Oz, over the rainbow and I thought I could be in love.

Paul had just turned 17. His birthday had been at the beginning of June. On our date we went for a walk, held hands and talked all about ourselves and our families. He had been devastated when his older brother who had been a Spitfire pilot had been killed flying during the Battle of Britain, and Paul said he too was going to join the Air Force and become a pilot as soon as he was old enough. I told him that my brother was serving in the Air Force overseas but hadn't been able to fly because of his poor eyesight. I loved our time together and we both said we wanted to meet again. Paul said next time he would try and scrounge enough money for us to go to the cinema; he was in the middle of taking his leaving exams but said he'd done all the studying he could do and wasn't too worried about it all.

We ended back at my home/hotel/barracks and I persuaded him to come in and meet Daddy. Of course we went in by the back entrance, past a couple of soldiers who did a double take and grinned at me coming in with Paul, and then into our very small living/dining room. Daddy got up from his chair and shook Paul's hand. He probably had reservations about me having suddenly acquired a 'young man' but he was his usual smiley niceness and made him welcome. He didn't stay long, it was about 7 o'clock in the evening and after all he still had to walk the three miles back to Sandsend. When I asked Daddy if he liked Paul, he said, 'He seems a very nice young man' –

then he said with a sort of sad look, 'But you're still my Ubs, aren't you?'

'Of course Daddy,' I said and we laughed and I hugged him.

When Mums came in from her job she asked about our day and I told her about my date and Daddy chipped in that 'he seems a very nice young man.'

We had some Supper, probably sausages (rationed) and mashed potato and then some cheese (rationed) and biscuits and when we'd cleared everything up I went up to my room, flung myself on my bed and knew I was just about the happiest, luckiest girl in the whole world. In the midst of all the horrible war and everything being messed up and worrying and sad, the best looking, nicest boy in the world, who only two days ago I didn't know existed, wanted to be with me. It was a bit like the feeling I had when I woke up on my 11th birthday and saw my beautiful bike beside my bed. Come to think of it, it was a lot like that.

Because of school and exams, at least until the summer holidays, Paul and I got together once a week on Friday or Saturday nights. The rest of the week was just longing for the weekend. If he could somehow get the money together we went to the cinema. In those days there was an unspoken rule that the boyfriend paid, even if he was still at school and penniless like Paul, which seems so unfair now but then it was part of a culture which saw the male as the provider/protector and the female perfectly happy with that and as far as I was concerned it was absolutely fine thank you very much. There was little or no talk of feminism, un-equality or thoughts of 'put downs' then, just a 'thank you' and a few kisses and hugs was enough. Occasionally we went to the Saturday night dance at the Spa which of course was crowded with all the Army people stationed in town. Paul wasn't a very good dancer but we managed to get around the floor pretty well and laughed a lot.

Paul would call for me, he would get the bus at least one way if he had the money, if he didn't, then he had to walk. I think there was the odd time he would get a lift with his father who was a local surveyor and had a car; as I've already said not many people did have cars then and anyway petrol was rationed. Maybe sometimes he would hitch a ride. If I wasn't quite ready Paul would chat to Daddy and once, as we left, he said, 'Maybe we should stay in with your Dad – are you sure he's okay?' I said, 'Oh yes, he's fine' – but I thought it was really nice that Paul was concerned for him and, well, as Daddy had said, he seemed a very nice young man, and he was.

That Summer went by happily enough in spite of news from the war zones not being very cheerful. A front had now opened up in the desert of North Africa, Germany having sights on the oil fields there and somewhere our troops were being trained in desert warfare; meanwhile I suppose it was good news that the Germans were suffering losses on the Russian front. After doing well in his exams, Paul had applied to join the Fleet Air Arm to train, as he had wished, as a pilot.

Back to school in September for my final year there – thank goodness! Needless to say Amy and June were not happy that I had acquired a boyfriend and came up with snobbish 'put-downs' such as they claimed to know Paul and his family and made stupid comments about them such as that they lived in a very small house and did I know his Mum had a job, so ridiculous when most wives, including my Mums, were working at something, either to make ends meet, or to help the war effort. So, as you can by now imagine, I just ignored them and tried to concentrate on my lessons which wasn't easy, especially Mother Maria's Early English History class given in her very knowledgeable, but really boring voice.

Christmas 1942 was very low key. Paul was waiting to hear when he would be called up and in the meantime was having driving lessons. We saw each other as often as we could and I wasn't looking forward to him going away. His present to me was a charm bracelet which I had admired in a shop window and I bought him a book called *A Man Called Peter* about a pilot who had flown in the Battle of Britain. Paul and I went First Footing which is a Northern tradition, calling at your friend's houses to wish them all a Happy New Year and get a piece of cake or something to drink. We kissed and hugged in the New Year at midnight and that was all – neither of us even hinted that we could take it any further and that's how it was then, innocence and restraint personified! And please, please, if there are any young people reading this, believe me, it was like that for most people and it really was fine, making plans, feeling close. It was enough that both of us just liked being together.

No-one spent a lot of money on presents but we did seem to gather together a lot, in each other's houses, talking, discussing the war, drinking lots of cups of tea and just feeling supported, I suppose. One evening, one of the officers who were then living in the hotel came through to our sitting room to visit with us. He was called 'Curly' – that was his nickname because he was completely bald! Well, he and my parents were talking about the war as usual and I suddenly wanted to give an opinion and excitedly butted in with whatever it was. Well, you would have thought a bomb had been dropped! Mums said 'Don't interrupt!' and even Daddy was scowling a bit so you can imagine I felt awful, yet a bit angry at the same time when, all of a sudden, Curly, who I will never, ever, ever forget, said: 'Hey folks, I'd like to hear what she has to say!'

Well, I was shocked. I looked nervously at Curly, looked at Mums and Daddy, stuttered a bit but managed to get out what I had wanted to say and they all, believe it or not, nodded, smiled and agreed with me. Wow! It was a big lesson to me that much as I loved my Mums and Daddy, they couldn't always get things right and that I could speak up other than when I was spoken to! You see at that time, children and even teenagers were expected to sit quietly and respectfully in adult company and actually ask permission to speak, as it was in most schools. It was okay to listen and take things in or to fetch and carry ('your legs are younger than mine!') and make yourself useful, but you were really not expected to voice opinions until you had left school or even until you became 21.

Although I know I was lucky with my background, upbringing and especially my parents, the custom that I've just told you about did play a part in an inability to express myself confidently for a long time. I knew what I felt and thought but had difficulty getting it out, afraid, I suppose of the reaction I would get. Again I don't blame my parents, they were just continuing the practice from their own childhood and how society was then. I believe that is how character flaws and social inadequacies are often passed on. Of course, finding a balance is what helps and encouraging young people to join in discussions to express themselves is fine, as long as they don't interrupt, disrupt, domineer or shout, with little respect or consideration for others which I believe does quite often seem to happen in today's schools and families.

In the Spring of 1943, just before his 18th Birthday, Paul left to join the Fleet Air Arm. He was soon to go to Canada to train as a pilot and said he would be away about six months. We had a last date and hugged and kissed and promised to write often; well actually, we said we'd write every day! Six months seemed like forever and I cried myself to sleep after we said our 'goodbyes'. His first letter to me began with the words 'My darling' which was so lovely and I thought how lucky I was, and also started my letters to him with 'My darling'.

Chapter 11

Very Mixed Feelings

OF COURSE I MISSED PAUL but felt good that we had met each other and I loved getting his regular airmail letters which were on the thin blue paper and combined envelope that we all used. I was working fairly hard studying for my final exams and glad that I would soon be leaving. Maureen and I were the only two to be sitting for the exams as the few who were around our age were evidently not considered ready including Amy and June. As I've said, Maureen was three years younger than me but at 13, was very bright and seemed also to have a photographic memory. I did so envy her ability to retain almost everything she read or heard.

Because I was the only one taking the Art exam, it was arranged for me to take it at the Grammar School which I wasn't looking forward to at all. On the day of the exam, I made my way up to the huge School buildings feeling really nervous and eventually found out where I was supposed to be. I didn't know any of the other students but they all knew each other and were chattering away happily so I felt a bit like a fish out of water. The person in charge showed me to a desk by the wall and then said for everyone to pay attention. She proceeded to tell us what we had to do and how much time we had. There was a selection of pencils and paints and a pot of water on the desk plus two large sheets of blank paper and at the end of the room a still life had been arranged which we were to paint in whatever style we chose. As soon as we were given the go-ahead to start, the room went quiet, heads went down, arms and pencils went up in hands waggling this way and that to get perspectives and to get on with the project.

I was quite happy once I got going on my 'work of art' when the boy in front of me suddenly turned around and with his elbow on the back of his chair knocked over my pot of water, which was by now a sort of brown muddy looking colour, all over my painting. Well, I let out a loud 'Oh no!' at which the supervising person came rushing over, everyone staring, boy-in-front saying 'sorry'; someone came with a cloth and started mopping away but my painting seemed all but ruined when it had been almost finished.

Well, we patted and blotted and the teacher person said it would be fine and not to worry – but how could I not worry? We were given two other items to work on but so much for a Pass Mark in Art, I thought as I trudged back home with a sad tale to tell my parents and the Art Teacher at St Marys (but probably to the delight of Amy and June). The thing was that as Art was really my best subject I had been depending on it as one of my Passes; my other exams were in History, Religious Study (or Scripture as it was called then), English Language, English Literature and Botany, and I was pretty sure I wouldn't pass in History (boring voice and all that). Anyway in the end when my results finally came popping through the letterbox at the end of August, lo and behold I had achieved my school-leaving Certificate and only failed in History as I was pretty sure I would. Amazingly enough I had a distinction in Art in spite of the muddy water episode, so all the worry had been for nothing.

I had had my 17th birthday in May and left school in July and had to decide what I was going to do next. Bets came home on leave, Aunt Nan had returned to live with Sarah, her sister at Havelock Place, leaving Uncle Bert and Audrey in London to cope with their jobs, their house there and the bombing. Bets looked great in her W.A.A.F. uniform and I really wanted to join one of the forces too but knew I would have to wait until I was at least 17 and a half. So what for now? I remembered that when I had been at Ambleside, we would walk to the town on Saturdays through a lovely park and as one of the main London Art Colleges was also evacuated to the Lakes we would see them sitting around the park in their groups, sketching and chatting and I thought how lucky they were to be just sitting around sketching in their rather funny, flashy clothes and a part of me must have decided that was for me, I would go to Art College when I left school; after all, it did seem to be what I enjoyed and did best.

I talked to Mums and Daddy about it and as usual they said okay. I bet they would much rather I stayed and got a job and helped out with a bit of much needed cash, but they wouldn't have said so and I honestly don't think it had occurred to me, self-centred teenager or what?!

The only Art College near enough for me to attend was 20 miles away in Scarborough and the earliest train left Whitby at 8:30 a.m. arriving there at 9:15. The college was about a mile from the Scarborough station so by the time I could arrive there it would be about 9:30 and half-way through the first class. Anyway it was that or nothing and the principal agreed I could go. All the other students lived in Scarborough so were busy sketching away or whatever before I arrived but they were all friendly and welcoming to me. The first day was a bit scary, like first days anywhere usually are, aren't they? But I was so happy to be finished with St Marys and loved the idea that I was an Art Student even though I wasn't lying around in a park in the Lake District under the trees, but as far as I was concerned it was the next best thing. I soon realised I had a lot to learn, but the main tutor was very patient, helping us to improve and particularly in taking time to find out what we were trying to reproduce. I found the classes in perspective really hard even when it was carefully explained and demonstrated, but when we were allowed the freedom to go mad with pencil or paint, then I was happy. Anatomy lessons with a skeleton and life drawing with a model were so new and interesting and I loved telling Daddy and Mums all about them when I got home.

    I soon got used to the routine, walking to the station every week-day morning which was about half a mile up the cliff, past the Metropole Hotel, the Sports Fields then left and along the road past where (uncle) Eric and (aunt) Madge lived, arriving at the station at around 8 a.m. in time to catch the Scarborough train. There were about four of us that caught it every morning, so we soon got together in the same carriage, (as trains used to have). Of course we were all travelling for our different reasons and the others were older than me, but it was nice to have their company. We didn't see each other on the journey home, all needing to return at different times. College finished at 4 p.m. but I had to leave early to catch the 4 p.m. train as there wouldn't be another until 6.

    One morning, I set off to catch the train as usual but as I turned from the side driveway of the hotel I was met by an amazing sight: there were hundreds, if not thousands of American soldiers just sitting or lying on the roadside along the length of the Promenade. They had evidently been brought overnight in trucks and were waiting to be housed. I had never seen an American before except in films of course, but they were all so friendly and jolly in spite of being dumped there probably cold and exhausted and for all I know maybe I was the first English girl they had come across. Anyway I just smiled at them as I made my way between their outstretched legs and kitbags, saying hello and that I hoped they would soon be warm and fed. Of course some of them were cheeky and said 'Can I come home with you babe?' but it was all friendly stuff and just another strange experience among the strangeness we were all facing

All that day I couldn't help wondering if they would all still be there when I got back home that evening but of course they had by then been dispersed to their various billets, in small hotels, halls, boarding houses and yes, even private homes around the town.

The Americans, along with their Jeeps and other military vehicles and equipment, were soon part of our little town's landscape, as well as all the British and Colonial troops who came and went as the war progressed. Occasionally I had started to go to the Saturday night dance at the Spa Ballroom which was always absolutely packed. Mums had made me a dress from parachute silk. I have no idea how she got hold of the material but maybe it was possible to buy left-over cuts from those who had a job in a parachute factory or something. I'm only guessing, you understand, but it had been dyed red and I loved it and it was my special dress for going out. I had also acquired a pair of high heel shoes which were also red – they had come from one of Mums' friends who was the same size as me.

I loved dancing with the Americans because they nearly all danced well, especially jiving which was such fun and we could all laugh a lot and forget about the war for a couple of hours. One problem was that at that time girls had to wait until they were asked by a guy to dance so it was a bit of a lottery whether you got to dance at all. Most of the girls about my age were like me and had a steady boyfriend who was in the forces and away so we didn't want to get involved with anyone – we just wanted to have a fun evening and to dance; so if we didn't get asked it was really disappointing. We weren't interested in drinking alcohol, apart from not being able to afford it anyway – well, it just didn't seem necessary. We loved being there, the music, the people, the atmosphere and we wanted to dance.

Once I was at the Spa dance sitting around the dance floor with some friends when suddenly a tall army chap appeared in front of me with a big smile on his face asking me for a dance. I looked up at him, surprised. I was used to sitting or standing around quite a lot, so trying not to jump up too eagerly, I said casually, 'Okay then' – and before I could hardly take a breath was being what I can only describe as 'whirled around' the floor at great speed, finishing up somewhere other than where we had started. By this time I was laughing so much and quite out of breath but so happy to be saved from an evening watching others dance, so I looked up at my rescuer and saw twinkling eyes in a sort of craggy face and lots of blond hair; and then the music started up again and it was slow this time, a song called 'I'll Get By'. He looked straight into my eyes, smiled and pulled me close to him and we started dancing again without saying anything and I had an overwhelming feeling of happiness and togetherness with this complete stranger.

This was confusing because I knew I cared so much for Paul, away in Canada who wrote loving letters to me every week and who I wrote to as well of how much I missed and loved him, which I did. Anyway we stayed together and after a while the dance came to an end with the traditional last waltz and he said:

'Can I take you home?'

There was absolutely no way I was going to say 'no'.

As you already know, the Spa wasn't very far from my hotel/barracks home but on the way there we managed to find out a lot about each other. He was from the North West of Scotland and although his name was Archie, he was called Mac. I told him my name but he insisted on calling me 'Kiddo' – I don't know why, maybe because he was 24 and I told him I was 18. Mac was in a special branch of the Army called the Mountain Regiment and had reached the rank of First

Lieutenant. I told him I was an Art Student but that I really wanted to join one of the forces.

We arrived at my door and I asked Mac if he'd like to come in and meet my parents, which he did. Daddy gave him a whisky and Mums and I had a cup of tea – I could tell they liked him. He stayed about an hour and when he left he didn't ask, he just said: 'I'll call for you tomorrow, I've got some time off, we'll go for a walk' – and he bent down and kissed me and then left. I shut the door in a bit of a daze. I didn't want to think about Paul, yet that didn't feel right – would it have been better to say 'no' to Mac? (Notice, I didn't say 'should'). For all I knew maybe Paul was meeting other girls in Canada or had even met a special one. That night I tossed and turned a lot and took a long time to go to sleep but I knew I would be going out with Mac the next day.

It was Sunday and we set off not really caring where we went. It was a lovely day, sunny but a bit breezy, and we just followed our noses. We held hands all the way and talked all about ourselves and what our lives had been like and what we thought about everything. Having walked around the edge of town so many times with Daddy I was able to show Mac the way and tell him about Whitby's long history. We went beyond the built up areas through the village of Ruswarp, by the river then across into Golden Grove, a woodland area leading back to the harbour and then back home. We must have walked about five miles in all but I didn't feel a bit tired because I knew, well, I just *knew* I was in love.

For the next few weeks I could think of very little else but Mac. No matter what I was doing, at College, on the train, at home, he was always on my mind. It wasn't particularly just a physical attraction since we seemed to agree on everything and feel comfortable with each other and laugh a lot. Once a week we went to the cinema in the evening and afterwards we would walk past the hotel and a short way up the cliff to sit for a while in one of the sheltered seats there, sitting very close, holding hands and looking out at the blackness that was the North Sea, sometimes hearing the waves surging in. We would hug and kiss and talk, but as I've already said and just like when I was with Paul, there was no going any further. In today's world, sex, by way of television, in films or videos, is everywhere, promoted, even pushed at people; but then, there was no television or videos and films were severely censored and definitely not allowed to be sexually explicit. Pregnancy outside marriage was a 'no-no' and seriously frowned upon. The contraceptive pill was way in the future and contraception of any kind wasn't spoken about as it is now. I remember that one night Mac was getting very passionate and suddenly pulled away from me and muttered 'Can't do this, it's not fair' and that was fine by me except I did briefly wonder why he said 'fair' and not 'right'.

I had become friendly with a girl called Mara who was a refugee from the Nazis in Germany. She was from a Jewish family who were still there but who had somehow managed to get Mara to England and she was living with a family I knew in Whitby who had asked me to be her friend. Mara told me a little about the Nazi attitude to Jewish people living in Germany and that she had had no contact with her parents since leaving them which sounded so terrible and made me realise even more of our need to win the war, even though we didn't know then just how monstrous that situation had become. Mac had a good friend called Tom who was also Scottish and stationed with him in Whitby; they had joined the Army at the same time. Mac and I decided it would be good for Tom and Mara to meet, so we arranged a blind date for them and the four of us went for a meal at a local café. We all got on really well and enjoyed the evening but I don't think Tom and Mara met again. Oh well, we all know, don't we, that we can't make things happen the way we would like them to.

I was still getting Paul's regular and loving letters and have to admit mine had become fewer and more difficult to write. He would be coming back to England soon, a fully qualified Navy Pilot with the rank of Sub-Lieutenant and I tried not to think about how things would be. I suppose we were all, without probably realising it, living one day at a time.

Anyway, it was May 1944, my first year at Art College was almost at an end and although we didn't know it, dear Mr Churchill and others in charge of our war efforts were planning an offensive and preparations were underway for the eventual move of allied troops across the English Channel to begin to free Europe on the day that would become known as D-Day. But at this moment in time Mac and I were planning to go to the Spa Dance on Saturday night and he was to call for me as usual. When I opened the sitting room door, Mac was already there and Daddy with a wry smile on his face suddenly reached in his top pocket for his handkerchief, and threw it across the room towards me.

'What's that for?' I said, laughing.

'Can't you guess?' he said and looked over towards Mac who was looking a bit miserable and who sort of mumbled:

'I've got my posting, I'm leaving tomorrow.'

I was used to people going away, but this was Mac and although I knew it was going to happen, my heart seemed to fall into my stomach and I just said:

'Oh dear,' or maybe it was, 'Oh no!' Well, it doesn't really matter, does it?

Hardly anyone used swear words then, well not like they do now and even if I'd known any I wouldn't have used one, but I felt lost for any kind of words. Mac just helped me on with my coat and we said 'Cheerio' and left.

As we gloomily walked towards the Spa, Mac said:

'There's something I need to tell you before I leave, but not now, later."

'That's really mean,' I said, 'Now I'll be wondering what it is all evening!' Secretly though I was thinking that maybe he was going to say he wanted us to be engaged before he left or something exciting like that.

We danced every dance and of course the band played our favourite song 'I'll Get By' but we definitely were not as carefree as usual and we didn't talk much. In the interval, Mac reached into his jacket pocket and produced an object which he said he wanted me to have: it was a Scottish kilt pin which he said was special as he had dug it up himself on the Island of Iona. He said that it was very, very old and he had always treasured it and wanted me to treasure it. That was nice, but I wondered why he didn't say then what it was he needed to tell me.

Eventually we were walking home and up the side driveway to the door when he stopped, took a step back and, very seriously said, 'What I have to tell you is...' He took hold of my hands. I could hardly breathe, then he said:

'Kiddo,... I'm married.'

In a flash, my world fell apart

'What?... Why? What? Why didn't you tell me before? I've only just got used to you leaving and now this, how could you, Mac?'

Well, there really wasn't anything more he could say except how sorry he was. It was pretty dark with only a half moon but I could see he looked sheepish and for a few minutes we just stood there.

I really couldn't take it in. It had never occurred to me that he might be married and it hadn't occurred to me to ask him. All I knew in a flash was that everything I had thought and felt about Mac, about us, was as nothing now. Whatever values I had, they definitely didn't allow for a romance with someone else's husband and as far as I was concerned, our goodbye would be for always.

A peck on the cheek was all I felt able to cope with. Then he said, 'I'll write Kiddo' and my heart felt so heavy. I said, 'Don't Mac' – and he walked away.

I ran inside. Daddy was still up and of course he thought my tears were only because Mac was leaving and made sympathetic noises and 'we all have to be strong' sort of comments. I didn't tell him, or Mums, that Mac was married. I felt a sort of shame about it in a way. I also had feelings for Mac's wife who had now become a shadowy figure in the background, yet at the same time I was envious of her; it was all very confusing when only a few hours before I had been so happy thinking that Mac was going to propose to me and we would possibly live happily ever after, but now that felt really stupid. How strange life can be. Suddenly I was heartbroken knowing that I was going to have to get over Mac and deal with the fact that we could never be together.

That night though, lying in bed, well, tossing and turning in it more like, I couldn't help wondering how he could have kept the fact that he was married from me when it was obvious, to me anyway, that we were falling in love. Had I only imagined that he felt the same as me? We had only known each other for a month but surely in all the times we had spent together he could have told me? Also I knew he must have been in touch with his wife and not told her about me. I just found it so hard to imagine how Mac, who had seemed to be such a decent, honest person, could have been so deceitful.

The next few days and weeks were hard. Much as I tried, I couldn't get the whole 'Mac' thing out of my head and I found it hard to concentrate at college; also, the Principal had been in touch with my parents to say that the 2nd year there would be much more intense and that I 'should' get lodgings in Scarborough so that I didn't arrive late and leave early. The way I was feeling then, I didn't fancy the idea of living on my own in Scarborough; maybe I wasn't really thinking too clearly about things but after talking it over with Daddy and Mums I decided to finish college for now or anyway at the year's end and see if it was still possible to join one of the forces. I suppose I thought that a complete change and maybe doing something to help in the wretched war would help me to get over Mac, I'm not really sure, but anyway that's what I decided to do.

The Gallery

The Hotel

Sketch of Princess Royal Hotel, Whitby

My brother Peter and 'fatty' me 1927

Mums 1937

Daddy 1937

My brother Peter, 1939

Whitby Bohemian Male Voice Choir, Seated Centre, William (WK) Waters, Vee's Father, my Grandfather

Peter and me, summer 1948

Daddy, mums, Bets and me on leave 1944

*1940. Evacuated to the Lake District outside Broadings.
From Left to Right: Joy, Irene, me, Maureen, Margot, Nancy.*

Looking after a 'young one' at Broadings, 1940-41, by steps leading to the woods.

Bets (Bride) in middle, Midge (R) and me (L) as bridesmaids, 1947.

Post-war photograph showing Crescent Garden & Promenade.

The Spa Theatre and Pavilion

Our Wedding

Chapter 12

1944 – Trying to be Grown Up

SINCE THE UNITED STATES had joined us in the war it had given a much needed boost to the whole operation, not just in manpower and weaponry but also our spirits and it was now looking as though a final offensive and victory were not far away. Of course nothing was certain and luckily for me, the Forces were still recruiting men and women to keep the numbers up and to make sure the whole thing was kept going until and beyond when peace came when there would be a lot of winding up and handing over to do. So it was that I walked into the Recruiting Office in town and volunteered to join the Women's Royal Naval Service. I was told I would have to go to Manchester within the next few weeks for an interview and medical exam prior to being accepted and that was that.

I knew Daddy didn't want me to join up. Mums seemed okay about it: she was so positive about everything, although I'm sure she had her worries and concerns about the way all our lives were being affected, as everyone was.

I had one of Paul's many lovely letters telling me he would be home within days. I was looking forward to seeing him but also really worried as I knew I felt differently towards him since Mac had been in my life. I wasn't happy about the way I felt but it had happened and I would have to deal with it.

For the next few days I was on tenterhooks not knowing when Paul might arrive. Our permitted entrance to the building, the back one, was only locked at night so anyone could walk in, and Paul did – suddenly, there he was outside our living room door, a big smile on his face and looking so excited and so handsome in his uniform. He didn't say anything, he just pulled me to him, wrapped his arms around me and kissed me. It was strange but I knew I didn't respond in the same way as I had before and Paul knew it, too. He said:

'What's the matter?'

I eased away from him and didn't say anything. It was obvious I wasn't as happy to see him as he had obviously and rightly been expecting. He backed away from me too and said:

'Have you been seeing someone else?' – his expression hurt and angry.

I nodded, feeling hopeless and ashamed and muttered, 'I didn't mean it to happen, Paul. Anyway, he was married and he's gone now. I didn't know he was married until just before he left. I still care about you so much; the last thing I wanted was to hurt you, I didn't want… I didn't mean it to happen.'

He didn't say anything, he just glared at me. I had betrayed his trust and our promises to each other and there was nothing I could do to change that. We stood in silence for what seemed like forever, then he turned and walked away. I knew his heart was breaking and I knew what that felt like. I ached for him and myself too. I cried a lot after he left but that didn't change anything, did it?

After a while Mums and Daddy came in and they could see I was upset so I told them the whole sad story about Mac, Paul and me, and of course they were sympathetic and kind and did their best to help me to feel okay about it all – but I didn't. At that moment I felt like I had messed up my whole life and Paul's too, maybe even Mac's and I became more aware that life could be very complicated.

The very next day I had a letter summoning me to Manchester for my Wrens interview and medical exam which was good timing as it helped to occasionally take my mind away from all the heartache.

Catching a train to Manchester was, for me anyway, quite an adventure. Of course it was then by steam train which chuffed its way through all the lovely Yorkshire countryside, stopping at every little village station along the way. Having to change trains at York, I eventually arrived at Manchester where I took a taxi to the recruitment offices.

Well, the interview didn't last long. A very smart Wren officer asked me a few questions, like why had I chosen the WRNS (I liked the uniform) and what did I hope to achieve (wanted to help); then she said there were only two occupations left to apply for, namely (1) Cooks and Stewards or (2) Aircraft Mechanic. Well, neither sounded what I had imagined being occupied with! Number one, I hadn't yet learned how to cook, having been brought up with a resident professional Chef most of the year who hadn't wanted me around, and Terry and Marian in the winter who had shared the cooking; I didn't know what being a Steward involved – it certainly didn't sound up to much; and as for Aircraft Mechanic! Well, I hadn't touched on any of that at Art College, had I? The woman could see I was floundering and said:

'There are a few openings for Security Messenger, secret documents have to be hand-delivered for safety purposes, how about that?'

I said, 'Yes, that sounds okay, I could do that.'

So that was it. After the medical exam, 'Ma'am' (that's what I learnt you have to call an Officer) told me I was accepted into the service and would soon hear when I would have to arrive at the Intensive Training Centre in Mill Hill prior to being posted .

I felt a bit deflated on the journey home but, well, I'd done it and would go along with whatever came up; after all, that's more or less what we were all having to do, and in a way I knew how lucky I was to be joining up at what seemed to be the tail-end of the war so had some idea what to expect. It was late when I arrived back home. Daddy met me at the station in Jo and was anxious to know all about the interview but I said I'd wait and tell him and Mums together, which I did and we laughed so much at the very idea of me being a Cook or especially an Aircraft Mechanic! The latter they thought was really hilarious but eventually they said they were sure I'd make a very efficient and trustworthy Messenger which cheered me up a bit as it wasn't what I had imagined doing as a Wren at all. In my dreams I would have been an Operations Plotter in a vast control room or at the very least secretary to an admiral or even Winston Churchill or, well yes, okay, okay! That was 'in my dreams' and I was 18 for heaven's sake!

Bets was on leave at Aunt Sally's and asked me to go to the Spa dance on Saturday with her so I said 'okay' but I didn't look forward to it as I had before. As we were making our way into the ballroom surrounded by the usual crush of people, I caught sight of Paul who must be still on leave. He was on the balcony with a group of his friends. I don't know if he saw me but if he did I knew he would probably ignore me which he did. I got asked to dance a few times and it was alright I suppose but when the band played 'I'll Get By' I couldn't help longing for Mac to be there and I just wasn't the same carefree girl I had been before he and I had met and the break up with Paul. I told Bets about it all and she didn't seem surprised or sympathetic and said, 'Well that sort of thing is happening to loads of people; times and things are not normal and won't be until the war's over' – which didn't exactly make me feel any better.

In fact it made me more impatient to get away and experience something different and to feel different, yet how strange when it would mean leaving the town, people and especially my parents that I loved so much. Growing up, or anyway trying to can be very confusing.

The next week I did receive instructions in the post to go to the WRNS training centre in Mill Hill which was on the outskirts of London. I knew Mums and Daddy had concerns for me but needless to say they waved me off at the station after lots of warnings and advice, tears and hugs. I suppose I was a bit apprehensive but also excited to be going off to something new, feeling in a very small way that I was joining in the war effort at last.

At King's Cross station I had been told to look out for a Navy truck which would take me to Mill Hill so I was relieved when I saw a Wren standing beside a transport truck and several other girls waiting just outside the station. Some of the girls must have been on the same train as me from York, not knowing that we were all bound for the same place. We all piled onto the truck and started chattering about who we were and what we had let ourselves in for.

We arrived at our barracks and tumbled out with our bags and baggage, followed our Wren leader inside and waited to be told where to go and what to do. After settling in we were sent off to the clothing store to get our uniforms which turned out to be quite a complicated operation such as getting the right sizes especially for hats and shoes. We were issued with one navy suit, one greatcoat, three shirts, one pair of shoes, a hat, three pairs of navy stockings (no tights then!), a tie, a shoulder bag and a regulation gas mask. We didn't get issue underwear – the WRNS was the only one of the three women's military services allowed to wear their own and most of us already knew this, and I guess we were a bit smug about it. We were told to change into our uniform straight away and attend the initial lecture that evening where we were left in no doubt about navy regulations, traditions and our responsibilities now we were members of the British Senior Service.

Even though we were on dry land we were to observe many of the same rules and terms used at sea. The floor was always to be referred to as the deck and making our sleeping area spotless, neat and tidy was called to lash up and stow! We were to keep our uniforms neat and clean and our hair forever above the collar of our jacket and never to pass an officer without saluting and of course with the correct salute, i.e. flat hand over the eyes as if gazing out to sea! We were also given strict instructions about hygiene and how NOT to get pregnant. Generally the message was that we were to uphold the reputation of the Royal Navy, be smart, sensible, keep calm and be prepared for anything. The uniform felt stiff and awkward at first but we were told the material loosened up with wear and constant pressing; the shoes too were pretty uncomfortable and after the first five-mile route march on the second day I had blisters on both feet. Every morning we had to assemble for drilling practice. I had seen hundreds of new recruits doing this in Whitby and giggled with friends about them being out of step; well, the joke was on me now, trying to keep up with my fellow beginners and the blisters didn't help.

Mac had been writing letters to me at home which had been forwarded. I hadn't answered them but knew he was still in England. In the latest one, I read that he was stationed at a camp near London and had given me a telephone number. After the first week at Mill Hill, we were allowed to go out for a few hours so rightly or wrongly, I made a decision to phone Mac just to tell him that I was now in the WRNS and where, but that I didn't think we 'should' stay in touch.

I felt so nervous, waiting for Mac to be found and come to the phone and when I heard his voice with it's slight Scottish lilt, all my moral determination to be cool and strong left me and I couldn't help telling him I missed him and that I would meet him on my time off at the weekend. Mac had also said how much he had been missing me and how much he cared; this was still confusing to me, knowing that he had a wife who I felt sure must miss and care for him too and presumably didn't know about me. Well, all I can say in my defence is that I was a bit dis-orientated, probably a bit homesick and felt I had to see Mac for what would probably be the last time one way or another.

We met in London at the Lyons Corner House café near Marble Arch. We hugged and just gazed at each other. It was wonderful and weird all at the same time; then, after a while, we had only just decided what we were going to order to eat when there was an announcement that a Buzz Bomb had been sighted on its way to London and we should all quickly go to the nearest air-raid shelter. Buzz Bombs, or Doodlebugs, were un-manned missiles which the Germans had been aiming at London for some time. Mac and I ran out of the building across the road and sheltered in what seemed like a sturdily built doorway, a short way down Park Lane. We could hear the strange buzzing sound of the bomb getting louder and just clung together hoping it would pass over us but still not wanting it to drop at all, anywhere. The sound cut out and a few minutes later we heard the awful sound of it hitting the ground not too far away. We stayed where we were for about ten minutes, not really knowing what to do but knowing things between us were different and somehow unimportant compared to bombs dropping and people not so far away being killed and injured. We went back to the café but of course it was closed, as more bombs could be on their way.

We walked for a while in Hyde Park, holding hands. Neither of us seemed concerned about more Buzz Bombs or our safety. We sat on a bench and I finally asked Mac how he could have kept his marriage secret from me. His explanation was that he had married his first girlfriend impulsively before joining the Army and that he cared for her very much but had fallen in love with me. Like me, he wasn't sure how it had happened and felt guilty; neither of us mentioned divorce – that wasn't something most people would even think about in 1944.

Basically, Mac and I knew we loved each other but couldn't do anything about it; it wouldn't have been right and I knew I couldn't have been happy knowing I had been the cause of a marriage break-up and someone else's unhappiness; after all, in a different way I had done that to Paul and I hadn't liked the feeling at all.

Mac was stationed at Lee-on-Solent and like me had come up to London by rail. We made our way back to the station and I walked with him to catch his train which left before mine. My heart was in my shoes and it felt like I was walking on it. We were standing beside a train that would take him out of my life forever when he said again, 'I'll write Kiddo,' and I said, 'Just stay alive and be happy, Mac.' We hugged, the guard's whistle blew and he jumped on the train and leaned out of the window, reaching out his hand to me. He wasn't smiling as he blew me a kiss and I stayed there waving, feeling an awful, empty, dull sadness. Then he was gone.

On the journey back to Mill Hill I felt just about as miserable as it's possible to feel. When I finally arrived back at the barracks, friends I had made in our first week of training were so bubbly and full of the fun they had had on their time off; I didn't think I could tell them how awful I was feeling – I just said I had met a friend and mentioned the Buzz Bomb which they had all heard as well.

That evening I telephoned my parents and told them I was okay. I didn't tell them I had seen Mac, or about the Buzz Bomb – I thought it might worry them; but going to bed that night and listening to the chatter of my roommates somehow helped to keep my mind from my heartache and before we said goodnight to each other we all said how lucky we were to still be alive and doing something, however small, to try to end the wretched war.

Chapter 13

Toughened Up

THE SECOND WEEK of training was all about continuing to smarten us all up and making sure we didn't avoid getting our hands dirty or complain about anything we were asked to do such as scrubbing floors, peeling hundreds of potatoes or at some point, in my case safely delivering papers by hand to Naval Headquarters in London to prove I was up to the job I had signed up for. Then there was all the drilling, route marches, lectures about our responsibilities, taking care of ourselves and looking out for our colleagues as well. Before we received our posting we were told that if we had any doubts about staying in the service and being able to do what was asked of us then we must be honest and leave. There were about a hundred of us new recruits and as far as I know there was only one who decided to leave.

At individual interviews we were asked if we had any preferred area we would like to be posted to, if it was possible. I said I would like to be 'somewhere up North' thinking it would be North of England only to discover I was going to the North of Scotland! It was somewhere called RNAS Rattray, a Fleet Air Arm training station about 50 miles from Aberdeen.

The journey from London to Aberdeen seemed endless; also, for most of the way it was very uncomfortable as, when I boarded at King's Cross station, the train was already crowded, mostly with service people and there were no seats available so the corridors, which ran alongside the compartments then, was where many of us had to stand or sit on our suitcases. The game was to hope someone with a seat would get off the train at one of the stations on the way and if you were quick you got the empty seat. Of course it helped if you were right outside a compartment door so a bit of shuffling went on if someone in the corridor got off as well or went to the loo. I eventually managed to get a seat at Edinburgh. It was bliss.

At Aberdeen there was a huge truck waiting to take any new arrivals to the base and several of us piled onto the back and onto the wooden benches, which weren't much more comfortable than suitcases, but hey! I was in the navy now and as I already knew, comfort wasn't exactly what it was all about. We were deposited at C-Camp and shown to our quarters which were Nissan huts housing eight people in bunk beds and with a wood-burning stove in the centre. Only two WRNS were in the hut when I arrived as although it was quite late, they explained that the others were on duty. One girl called Sheena showed me where the toilet and washing area (the Heads) was and filled me in on just about everything else; she also went with me to the Canteen to get a cup of tea and a bun which was all there was as the Galley (kitchen/dining area) was closed. Sheena told me there were three camps at the base, A, B and C, and she reckoned C was the worst and she was trying to get a move to A-Camp which was closer to the Airfield where she worked in the Control Tower. We had to keep our clothes in our suitcase under the bunks; mine was a bottom bunk but after a while and as people moved out you got elevated to a top bunk. That first night I crawled into mine and in spite of Sheena's helpfulness I cried into the pillow feeling overwhelmed with it all and missing my parents and everything I was used to and well, just cold and miserable. Tomorrow, I would cope.

Next morning I was woken early by the other girls getting ready for their morning watch. I'd been told already that I must report to a senior officer to receive instructions so I thought I might as well get on with it and get ready. I knew where the Galley was now and as I was starving I made my way there to get some breakfast. The mug of tea was good but the fried spam and a 'doorstop' of fried bread wasn't exactly pre-war Princess Royal Hotel standard but it filled my tummy. I sat with and talked to another girl about the life there and she said it was bleak and very isolated and as it would soon be midwinter, very cold. We were allowed a certain amount of fuel for our stoves but as I soon discovered if we ran out of coal or wood we would burn anything deemed to have little value, just to keep ourselves warm.

There was only one other Messenger on the base and along with her my job was to collect, sort and deliver all inter-station communication. We had a tiny office, a hut, but no transport, so we had to catch the inter-camp bus which occasionally toured the whole area and which had to wait for us each time we got off to make a delivery. The other Messenger was called Mhairi (pronounced Vaari) which she told me was Gaelic for Mary and which I immediately decided that if I ever had a daughter, that is what I would call her – I thought it was lovely. We didn't actually see much of each other as we shared the work, handing over as each watch ended. Our little hut had a stove to heat it, but as we regularly ran out of fuel it could be verrrry cold. There was a kettle, stuff to make a mug of tea, a sink and a table on which to do our sorting and a chair and that was it.

My first day was once again like first days of anything, anywhere, a bit nerve-racking but I soon fell into the routine and got to know lots of people around the station and where everything was. I particularly enjoyed stopping off at the Control Tower where Sheena would usually give me a big 'Hello' and introduce me to what was effectively the hub of the whole station and when we were back in our hut we would chat about it all and giggle especially if we rather fancied one of the guys there. Rattray was a training Airbase for qualified pilots to get used to flying the Swordfish which was a plane used on Aircraft Carriers; they called it a Stringbag because it looked and felt like it was held together with string – not very helpful to the young men learning to fly them in difficult conditions!

Anyway, one day when I was at the Control Tower, Sheena showed me the list of pilots due to start training the following week. I could hardly believe my eyes when whose name should (sorry!) DID I see there but my Paul's! Well, I know he wasn't 'my' Paul anymore but I was so looking forward to seeing him and surprising him that I was a WREN now and that I was right there for heaven's sake! However, I didn't know how I could contact him as he would be living in the officers' quarters; I just hoped I would bump into him one day or maybe at the weekly Saturday night dance. Well, I was in the middle of my mail-sorting one morning when who should appear at the door of my little hut but the man himself, lovely Paul and with a big smile on his face at surprising me. I don't know how he had found out I was there and I'm sure he probably told me, but sorry, I can't remember that and it's not really important. We didn't hug or anything. I made him a cup of tea and although we chatted a bit he didn't ask to see me again and I realised he had moved on and although friendly enough seemed almost indifferent to me. I suppose I was glad for him; my feelings were sort of mixed, disappointed I guess, but having to accept that Paul was lost to me, we had both changed and our lives had changed too. I didn't see him again until after the war when we were both back in Whitby. I'll tell you about that later.

One night when Sheena and I were huddled around the stove after work, she told me that a Radio Telegraphist in the Control Tower was moving to another station and they would need a replacement, and why didn't I apply? Well, I didn't know it was possible to change jobs like that but was excited at the thought that I might be able to work right in the heart of everything like Sheena. She told me where I needed to go to ask about it and as it was one of the offices where I delivered mail I decided to do that the next day.

Of course I had no idea how to be a 'Radio Op' but Sheena said the other girls there would show me and that it wasn't difficult to learn the ropes. I had found things quite relaxed once you were established at a Fleet Air Arm Station; unlike the Navy 'proper', all the strict rules that had been drilled into us at Training were not so rigidly enforced at Rattray; also we were allowed to wear Bell-Bottom trousers like the men and the easy slash-neck shirts, and as long as our hair was neat and tidy the officers didn't seem to mind if it was long enough to reach our collar. Of course, we smartened up to go to the Saturday film or the dance or Sunday Divisions (Church).

I could hardly believe how easily I was transferred from Messenger to trainee Radio Telegraphist pending – in less than half an hour in fact! Of course I had to keep up my postal job until they brought in a replacement, but as I had been granted leave in about three weeks' time over the Christmas period I would start my new job when I returned. Sheena and I hugged when I told her – she was so pleased for me; we had become good friends and I was so looking forward to being part of the Control Tower crew and out of my rather lonely Post Office hut.

As December arrived, and being in the very north of Scotland, snow started to fall and getting around the camp even on my bus-delivering journeys became really difficult. We tried to keep our stove burning overnight in our cabin to keep warm; we took it in turns to keep watch over the fire and to find any kind of fuel for it. At some point we took charge of a very young Manx (no tail) cat who found its way to our door; we kept it fed from our left-overs and took it in turns to let it out and to sleep on the end of our beds. We called it 'Maxi'.

We gave Maxi lots of love but when I got back from my Christmas leave she had disappeared – that's cats for you!

I was so excited to be going home for Christmas but the journey turned out to be both awful and wonderful. There were no spare seats as usual, so out in the corridor once more was I; then, somewhere between Aberdeen and Edinburgh there was an air raid warning so of course the train had to stop where it was with all its lights out as was the wartime way of things and wait for the 'all clear' which meant I missed my connection at Darlington. It was by then late at night when I stepped onto a deserted Darlington station platform, not a living soul in sight and the office and everything dark and closed, until lo and behold I caught sight of a light at the far end of the platform and started walking towards it tugging my suitcase. As I got near I could see the light was from a little hut and a figure appeared in the doorway calling out to me: 'Hello! Are you alright?' A man in a dark blue uniform walked towards me and I realised he was a Salvation Army member. I told him I was stuck, with no connection to Whitby until (I hoped) in the morning whereupon he closed up his hut and said, 'Don't worry my dear, I'll take you to our hostel for the night' – and he insisted on carrying my bag.

Well I couldn't believe my luck or the kindness offered to me and trotted along beside my Good Samaritan until we came to the hostel, and went inside where there was a fire blazing away and a made-up bed right beside it. I was told to make myself comfortable and brought a cup of tea – unbelievable! I then had a good night's sleep and was wakened next morning in time to walk to the station. I offered what little money I had but was told that wasn't necessary. Needless to say I have never forgotten the help and kindness that cold night and never fail to support any fund raising by the wonderful Salvation Army and their true Christian spirit.

It was another strange Christmas. Mums said I had put on rather a lot of weight which I hadn't really noticed, but she was right: when I tried my 'civvy' clothes on they were definitely on the tight side. It wasn't surprising really as I had been comfort-eating the stodgy food in the galley, which I ate because I seemed to be always hungry. I made a mental note to eat less and get back to my pre-wren small size.

There was yet another regiment in the hotel, and using the first floor as offices so all the furniture from there had been stowed away on the top floor. One day we watched as a large truck drove out of our driveway stacked up with our beds and other furniture; we had no idea where it was going but we never saw any of it again. Although Daddy must have worried about things like that, and the future, if we had any that is, especially at times like that, during those wartime days you just didn't think too much about losses, as everything was for winning the war.

It was so good to be with my parents again and catch up on their lives and I told them what I could about my Navy life and met up with their friends and some of my own. We had a lovely Christmas Day meal as Mums had been saving up their coupons to buy a large bird and a Christmas pudding and we went 'first-footing' on New Year's Eve.

We ended up the evening at Madge and Eric's and it was well after midnight when suddenly there was a shattering sound which we all knew was a bomb having fallen very close by. The windows rattled and we all froze; then 'Young Eric' who was home on leave went to the front door and told us the Metropole Hotel which was housing hundreds of Army personnel was on fire. The Hotel was only yards from where we were and we all donned coats and dashed out to see if there was anything we could do. The Fire Service and First Aid people were soon there and telling us to stay back so we went slowly and rather shakily back to the house. The next day we heard that casualties had been surprisingly low as the bomb had landed to the side and rear of the Hotel with only a small amount of damage. Anyway it was certainly a shock start to the year 1945. I haven't told you but there had been other bombs dropped on the town usually from German aircraft returning from raids on the industrial areas further North and presumably jettisoning left-overs rather than taking them back. So although the suspected invasion of our coastal area didn't materialise, Whitby like anywhere in the country needed to be alert to random attack.

My leave was soon over and it was back to Scotland and my new job. Arriving back at C-Camp after the long journey, standing most of the way as usual, I flopped on my bunk and asked the two other girls, Isa and Hazel, where Sheena was, only to be told that she had finally moved to A-Camp which she had been trying to do. I really missed her even though all the others in my hut were so friendly and nice and we all helped each other, but Sheena and I had really clicked in a giggly, silly, fun sort of way. Another of the hut-mates, Rosie, had been de-mobilised and left her shirts and other uniform and stuff for us to share out; also, she had been in the bunk above me so I got to move up in the world, so to speak; this was great but I decided I would still also try and get a move to A-Camp even if I couldn't be in the same hut as Sheena. It made sense to be near the Control Tower where I was going to be working. Also I really missed Maxi to stroke, feed and curl up on my bed at night but hiegh-ho, nothing stays the same, does it? You think you've got things sorted then bingo, you haven't! Well, of course you certainly haven't when there's a war on and you're in the forces.

I carried on for another couple of weeks doing my postal job whilst waiting for a replacement and an official notice to say I could start Radio-Op training; then, in what seemed like no time, I was installed in the lovely, open, operations office with its huge windows overlooking the airfield and learning the drill of communication with the pilots before and after they scrambled (took off) until they were three miles distant when the Wireless Ops would take over. The same routine occurred for their return, when they would re-connect with us three miles from the airfield until they were safely pancaked (landed). I very soon got used to it and absolutely loved it. The first job on the a.m. watch was telephoning around all the other Naval Air Stations to check on their weather conditions and report to the on-duty training and flight officers. I did wonder if Paul might be one of the pilots I would be communicating with which would have been fun, but he didn't appear so I assumed he had finished his time at Rattray and left which was confirmed for me by one of the training officers, so that was that.

It was such a light hearted atmosphere in the Tower between operations, probably because we needed to relieve the tension we all felt during 'action stations'. There was a period when two of my fellow R.T.'s were ill and I had to stay in post over a triple watch period, basically 24-hours. I won't say it was a piece of cake, but nothing awful happened and I managed to stay awake but, oh, what joy it was to get back to my bunk and sleep and remind myself that those at the front line of enemy action would be doing that regularly and maybe not even surviving for a good sleep.

There were some great crazy moments too, like when one of the training officers called John took me for a ride round the airfield perimeter in his MG sports car one day when bad weather had halted operations, and he let me get in the driving seat and virtually taught me how to drive. Round and round we went, the perimeter at the time being clear of any vehicle, aircraft or obstruction and it felt so safe and free and fun. Actually our nickname for this guy was 'The Hon John' because we knew he had some sort of title but that didn't impress us one bit and he was just one of us anyway; okay, he did try to more than kiss me but I soon put a stop to that! I knew the Hon John was a married man and I wasn't going down that road again thank you very much, even though I knew he probably expected a special kind of 'thank you' for my little jaunt; well, that's what he got, the word 'thank you' (I even added 'very much'!) and we stayed good friends.

I now saw Sheena regularly at work and it wasn't long before she told me there would soon be a place in her hut and I could apply to move over to A-Camp. I had found out that moving around really wasn't a big problem and the 'powers that be' were glad to help us settle and be as happy as possible in our work and living conditions as life was pretty grim on such an isolated station like Rattray as we were almost completely confined to the base.

Moving is always a bit of an upheaval but I caught the inter-camp bus with all my stuff. It was a bit hard saying 'goodbye' to Isa, Hazel and the others and my top bunk but I was glad to be re-uniting with Sheena and making more friends. A-Camp was definitely nicer and better equipped than C. The hut was larger and there was a huge stack of firewood to feed the stove. Even though spring was on its way it was still very cold in the North of Scotland and sitting around the stove at night was one of our main occupations, talking and sharing our stories with a mug of tea. I soon got to meet my new hut-mates and, as before, they were almost all Scottish and one girl called Jeanie was from a place called Kirkcaldy in Fyfeshire and her accent was so strong I really had difficulty understanding her – but she was very sweet natured and had a lovely sense of humour; she would make some hilarious remark and while they were all laughing I would ask them, 'What did she say?' Then by the time they interpreted for me I would start laughing after they had all finished. They didn't seem to have any trouble understanding me which seems strange when you think about it.

We would all get clean and smartened up for Saturday nights when we would have either a dance or a film in the big hall which was in A-Camp and once a month we could catch the service bus to Aberdeen. I only did that once because we had so little money that all we could do there was walk around the town and maybe have a cup of tea or something in a café. I suppose it was a change of scene but that was about all. The bus got a bit noisy on the journey home because most of the lads had had a few drinks and got a bit cheeky with us but we gave back as much as we got and it was all good clean fun. One day when I was off duty and bored, I borrowed Jeanie's bottle of peroxide and made a blonde streak in my hair from the parting right down one side – mad really, but it was a bit different and I kept it till it finally grew out.

One of the films we had was called 'State Fair', an American musical, and it was so jolly and different from our own lives in England at that time that it sort of lifted our spirits and we were all humming the songs afterwards and trying to copy the dances. I got to know one of the trainee pilots one time at the dance – he was called Tony, and while he was at the base we met up several times. He was a really sweet young man and he managed to get me an officer-issue kitbag from stores which was a really nice zipped travel bag not available to us OR's (other ranks). I was so thrilled with it! I knew some of the other girls had managed to scrounge one and wished I could get one too instead of my heavy suitcase but you had to know an officer who was prepared to say he needed one. The longer you were in the Services, you got to know all the little things you could do or get to make life a bit easier. Tony was a riot with his mates – they all seemed to like to rib him a lot because he was a bit shy and sensitive but he was such a good sport; he took it all in his stride and they loved him for it. He was shy with girls too and consequently with me, so there wasn't really much kissing or cuddle action between us, but we were friends and remained in touch long after he left Rattray

I suppose I could (not 'should') mention that my pay for the rank of Ordinary Wren was fifteen shillings a week, about 75 pence in today's money. We received it every two weeks so it seemed quite a lot at one pound and ten pence (£1.50). It must seem so little compared to today's wages and cost of living since inflations and de-valuation of the pound, but after all we had hardly any expenses, our lodging, food and clothing all being provided, and also, we received travel vouchers for getting home leave. Extras or personal items were available on the base at low prices and none of us smoked.

Not long after I had started working as an R.T. Op. I applied for and was given the rank of Leading Wren; this was fairly automatic unless you were useless and I didn't meet anyone who was. Wrens had to be hard-working, willing and generally helpful or they didn't become Wrens. It seems hard to believe, but I honestly can't remember if I got a pay rise with the promotion but it wouldn't have been much and anyway didn't seem important. A few weeks later I was summoned to the admin office and asked if I would be interested in being commissioned. It was a shock since I have absolutely no idea why I was considered capable of that and definitely didn't feel up to it and said sorry but I really didn't feel ready. Although I was prepared to do anything I was asked to do, I didn't feel confident enough then, as I saw it, to tell others, especially my mates what to do.

Since the combined Allied Forces had started their offensive to free German-occupied Europe on D-Day in June 1944, we were getting news that it was going well and there was a feeling around the camps that just maybe the war would soon be over. The snow stayed with us into February, followed by strong gales and rain through March causing poor flying conditions most days; but April finally arrived and we could actually do without the stove on in our hut. There were no trees to blossom in that part of Scotland and no spring flowers to bloom in our mostly grey, concrete camp, but somehow our wartime home began to seem less dreary and I had learnt that those who inhabited that space had made it so. No matter where you are and however dull or uncomfortable, if you are with good people you can be happy. Or perhaps put another way, it's people who make a place, or don't.

Chapter 14

War Ends – New Beginnings

ON THE 8th OF MAY of that year, 1945, Germany finally surrendered to our Allied Forces and the war in Europe was over. We whooped and jumped around and hugged each other and our dance on Saturday that week was a joyous one. Of course, along with the Americans, we were still at war with Japan and many of our captured service and other people were still in captivity and as we eventually found out being treated badly. Attention now turned to also bringing that area of conflict to an end.

At the end of May the 26th I turned nineteen and one of my cabin-mates Esme who was a cook made me a cake. We couldn't find any candles but it was a treat for us all and I had cards and some money from home. I still had airmail letters from Mac but I couldn't bring myself to write back and it was really hard when he sounded desperate to keep the relationship going and I could tell he was still in an area of conflict, but my head told me not to write back, so there we are, or I suppose were.

It was one evening in July I think during a late watch, when during a break, I was sharing a mug of tea with the duty officer when he said, 'I just heard, we've split the atom!' Completely puzzled, I said, 'What on earth does that mean?'

'It means,' he said, 'the release of nuclear energy and the possibility to make a very powerful bomb, so powerful that it could bring an end not only to this war, but to all war, a deterrent in fact.'

Having little or no scientific knowledge or even insight, I still didn't understand until a month later, in August, when we learnt that two atomic bombs had been dropped on two cities in Japan causing huge devastation and the Japanese to surrender. It was a horrible end to the war, but the war itself was horrible and had taken such a terrible toll over the past six years and it had not been caused by those who had to make the decision to end it.

We did celebrate the night we heard that the total war was over. It became known as VJ Day whereas the victory over Germany had been named VE Day. We made a big bonfire, even throwing some of our chairs and tables on it; we guessed we wouldn't need them for much longer and they were like matchwood anyway. Needless to say there was some alcohol floating about and the noise and singing and kissing was all around us. I think some hardy souls stayed up around the bonfire all night, but most of us wandered back to our bunks soon after midnight; we didn't sleep much though, talking about how much longer we would be Wrens and what our lives would be like in peacetime.

The next day we were all summoned to a talk by the Station Commander, basically that we were to carry on as normal until we heard anything new. He did say that in time there would be some movement of personnel possibly posting to other bases and re-training for other trades as many of those serving in the regular Navy overseas would be coming back and taking over the work we had been doing.

Training of our young volunteer pilots was being wound down and operations in the Control Tower became a matter of our just being there. There was a light-hearted atmosphere everywhere in the camps though and we were all more or less ready for what and wherever we were going to be. I had news from home that my brother Peter would be back very soon, and also that cousin Harry had been released from his prisoner of war camp, both after being away for almost six years. There were going to be so many homecomings and reunions, joyous yes but maybe for some also difficult. The world had after all been turned upside down; so many lives had been lost, others forced to change and adjustments would not always be easy, just another price to pay for gaining freedom from aggression.

And so the day came when I was summoned, along with several others to learn my fate about re-training, new posting and what and where I was heading. Lo and behold, it was back to Yorkshire, to a town called Wetherby, about 70 miles from home albeit only temporarily to train as a Writer, the Navy term for a secretary. The course was for a month and we were to be granted two weeks' leave prior to it starting. Sheena had asked to stay at Rattray as her home was near Aberdeen so she would stay until her time for discharge. Several of the Scottish Wrens had also asked to stay there until their time to leave the service; most had been in longer than me and would soon be due for discharge anyway.

It was a dull, foggy day in September 1945 when I climbed onto the back of a Navy truck, similar to the one I had arrived in a year before, heading first for home which I hoped would be really ours once more, seeing Peter and hearing all about his time away, future plans of Daddy and Mums, getting the Hotel going again – goodness, there would be so much we could now talk about and then I would be off to learn another new job, to new places and people and, well, it was all quite hard to take in and exciting.

On the other hand I had very mixed feelings about leaving RNAS Rattray. It had been an amazing experience for me and I had learnt so many things, mostly how to accept whatever situation you're in however complicated or challenging and make the best of it. The people I had lived and worked with had been true friends and I would never forget them and their combined ability to overcome any difficulty or hardship with humour, co-operation and kindness. But it was over and the reason for our coming together had ended and saying my 'goodbyes' was hard, so we had tried to make them light-hearted 'see you in Hell you grotty old thing you', that sort of thing, especially as we knew we probably wouldn't ever see each other again. Well, 'that's life' as they say and goodbyes have featured a lot in mine; moving on can be both exciting and sad and, as I said, the cause of very mixed feelings.

At least there was now no chance of train delays due to air raid warnings and I actually had a seat in a compartment for the whole train journey to Whitby, whoopee! I was so surprised when my brother Peter met me at the station in 'Jo'. Of course, he had been driving in the RAF and of course he was surprised to see me 'all grown up', as he said. I had been 13 when he left. Our little family was together again and that night we had so much to talk about it was after midnight when we finally went to bed.

I noticed Daddy's hair wasn't dark any more – it was silver and even though he was happy that we were, however briefly, all together again, I could tell the wartime years and difficulties had taken their toll and he sometimes seemed to be distant from us. Mums was her usual jolly self but she too sometimes looked strained and seemed much thinner than before. Peter was full of his future career plans to study optics and become an Optician. He had already made arrangements to do this with some of his RAF redundancy money. I could tell Daddy was disappointed that Peter had no wish to stay and become involved in running the hotel and maybe he then thought maybe that could be the future roll for me, but rather like not having been ready to be considered for a commission, I didn't feel ready to agree to that either.

Previously it had been almost automatic that sons or daughters would enter a family business as they left school and were rarely given a choice in the matter, but now it was different: young people had been forced to move away from the expected behaviours and traditions of the past and were motivated to follow their own ideas and to be adventurous. Whilst I didn't have any particular goals in mind, I believed there were options to think about. Daddy could tell, I feel sure, that neither Peter or I was keen on supporting them in the future of the hotel and if I felt bad about that then, I feel worse now when I think of how they had lived through the years of seeing the hotel deteriorate and had hoped for the possibility of our help to restore it only to be turned down; it must have been such a disappointment but they took it with the good grace that they seemed to do about everything.

The hotel was a complete mess. It was heartbreaking to walk around what was by now an almost empty shell, bare floors, goodness knows where the carpets had gone, but they would, I'm sure have needed replacing anyway and just everything, everywhere looked so dejected and worn out – a bit like it's newly re-united owners. I believe they received about £2,000 in compensation but even then, that barely covered the cost of redecoration which was needed inside and out. Because my parents had always seemed to take everything in their stride so to speak and, looking back on my 19-year-old feelings at the time, I realise that I just assumed they would sort it all out somehow and by the time I came out of the WRNS the hotel and our lives would just carry on as it had been before the war. So it was that when my leave ended, I left them thinking all would now be well and my mind was mostly on my new course and future posting with hardly a thought for my desperately worried parents and the enormous task they faced to repair both their home and business.

Arriving at Wetherby station, I was met and ushered into the Station Waiting Room where there were about 12 or maybe 15 other Wrens all apparently like me about to be re-trained and waiting to be transported to the base. We had to wait until all the expected trainees had arrived so I managed to squeeze myself into almost the only remaining sitting space and join in the chatter. Eventually we heard another train arriving. The door opened and two more Wrens came in. We all shuffled along trying to make room for them to sit and one came over to sit next to me. She was very attractive-looking with soulful eyes and a lovely smile and she immediately started talking to me. I told her my name and she said hers was Barby. We stayed together as we all piled onto the back of the truck and stayed together for the remainder of our time in the service, afterwards becoming good friends, which you will find out about later as I move swiftly on.

The accommodation at our training camp was pretty good. We each had our own small room in a long building of about ten rooms with The Heads at one end for which there was a bit of a scramble every night and morning. We were instructed in basic secretarial duties, filing and the importance of keeping accurate records, etc., lots of lectures from our Naval Instructor on what was or wasn't acceptable in the Royal Navy. It was like being back at our basic training again and believe it or not we had a route march and practice drill twice a week. After the day's work we would sometimes pop down to Wetherby town centre and use the phone box in the High Street to phone home and then maybe have a snack in one of the cafés. It gave us time to chat and usually have a moan about our instructor who we thought was a bit of a misogynist as he wasn't very nice to any of us and we couldn't think why, as we were all doing everything he asked us to do.

Barby and I chatted a lot, usually at night before bedtime. She was a Yorkshire girl like me except from Bradford in the industrial West of the county and her Father was something important in the Wool Industry. She was engaged to an American GI called Dan and had a diamond engagement ring and a photo of him always by her bedside and I thought he looked lovely and rather envied her, but she told me that her Father wasn't happy about Dan as he didn't seem to approve of him. I said if she was in love then she must follow her heart – me being the true romantic, remember? Barby was just a few months younger than me and since she joined the WRNS had been stationed at Bletchley Park which she told me was top secret and so obviously couldn't tell me anything about it. Of course we all know now about the de-coding research and work that went on at Bletchley and which made such a vital contribution to the war effort. I told her about Rattray and my own disastrous love-life and she sympathised and said I had done the right thing (about Mac).

Our month at Wetherby seemed to take forever but at last we were told we had 'passed' and where we were to be posted. Barby and I were happy when we found we were both going to the same place, Lowestoft in Norfolk, another packing up, another train journey, another billet. This time we were stationed in what pre-war had been a Bed and Breakfast Terrace house right on the sea front which we thought was really nice and for me a bit like being on the seafront at home. Our workplace was in what was called the Crows' Nest which was a group of office buildings at the bottom of a deep gorge. Most of the work was typing and in the afternoons we found it difficult to keep awake, something to do with the low location I suppose but we were always relieved when it was time to leave and climb back up all the steps and to the fresh sea air. I had been used to working eight-hour watches at different times of the day or night at Rattray, so it was a nice change to be working regular day-time hours. However, Barby and I hadn't been in Lowestoft very long, about four months when we received orders to relocate to Chatham Barracks in Kent. Actually, as the weather in winter on that East coast was, as at Whitby, inclined to be very cold and wild, we didn't mind the move a bit further South. Apart from going to a few dances, walking along the seafront and into town a few times, we hadn't really settled in or got to know the area or made many friends, so it wasn't so hard to move on again for what we guessed may be our final posting.

I had been hearing from Tony, my young pilot friend at Rattray and just before we were due to move to Chatham, I had a letter from him asking me to a big station Dinner Dance at the Fleet Air Arm base in Cornwall where he was now stationed. He said it would be a posh affair and I would need a long dress. Well I didn't have a long dress but was thrilled to be invited and really wanted to go so I phoned home to Mums to ask if she could send me one of her dresses and she said she would. Well, I got permission for a weekend leave and a voucher for the journey and as I had told Mums where to send the dress to Cornwall, off I went full of excitement and anticipation. Tony was there to meet me from the train and it was so good to see him and his cheery face, but guess what? No parcel containing a long dress had arrived, so feeling very down-hearted, I thought that was the end of me going to the 'posh do'. Tony took me to the base anyway, and showed me where I would be staying in the Wren officers' quarters, as I wasn't there as an Ordinary Wren but as a private guest. He introduced me to three of the officers who knew about me and the non-arrival of the dress, then, what a surprise when these lovely people took me under their wing and said they would definitely find something for me to wear and wouldn't think of me 'not going to the ball'. What a hilarious time we had, as one of the officers who was a similar shape and size to me came up with a white dress with a red poppy design all over it which I absolutely loved, and which they virtually pinned me into as it was a bit big around the waist now that I was thankfully back to my normal size; then they also had to pin it up all round the hem but it did look pretty good.

The evening was really lovely, very formal in the large Mess Hall, the officers all in their dress uniforms with many family and other invited guests. It was a belated celebration of the end of the war. There were quite a few jokes going around about my Cinderella-like situation but it was good fun and I got to know and dance with lots of Tony's handsome friends including the Station Commander who said he had spent time at Rattray and knew how grim it could be. Tony was as popular with his mates there as he had been in Scotland and was persuaded to perform his special trick which was sitting on the floor and crossing both feet behind his head; he was double jointed, I suppose, but it never failed to impress everyone even at such a 'posh do'!

The next day he took me to the little seaside town of Fowey which was so quaint and pretty and we walked down to the sea and had tea in a harbour side café, talking and laughing a lot. The setting and the occasion was so romantic but I guess dear, sweet Tony wasn't the romantic type or too shy or whatever, and just seemed to want us to be friends. My exciting weekend was soon over and it was time to catch the train back. It was a 'peck on the cheek' goodbye from Tony as I gave him a big 'thank you' hug. I did feel a real affection for him and we agreed to see each other again when we could manage it.

Back in Lowestoft Barby was all agog to hear about my weekend and I enjoyed telling her how the Wren officers had been so great in their determination to fix me up with a dress and tried to explain that Tony wasn't really a 'boyfriend', just a friend. She seemed disappointed and said:

'Why do you think he asked you to go all that way if he doesn't have feelings for you?'

'Well,' I said, 'I'm not sure myself but we're good friends, Barb. If the "flame" isn't there, it isn't there, is it?'

'Did you think it was there?

'Well to be honest Barb, I really miss having a Paul or a Mac in my life and Tony is such a lovely guy. I do think love can develop from friendship so I gave it a chance. I suppose it just isn't meant to be but we're still friends. Anyway I fancied going to a posh dance and I really enjoyed it, so there.'

Of course the parcel with Mums' dress would eventually arrive in Cornwall so I had asked for it to be re-addressed back to me, and then I would send it back to her. What a carry-on!

The following week we packed up and set off for Chatham. We found we were to be billeted in Rochester, a few miles from the barracks, in a large house which in peacetime was the Deanery to the Cathedral there. I suppose it had been requisitioned by the War Office, just like our hotel had been. Goodness knows where the Dean was living if there was a Dean during wartime. We were told there was a lot of history to the building and although our sleeping quarters were empty except for our bunk beds and a couple of chairs, we could see what an architecturally beautiful house it was with elaborate architraves and huge ornate windows. Actually, as there were only a few of us living there it could be a bit spooky at night; also, there was no heating or hot water, and although we were used to that, I did feel nostalgic for Rattray, where we had made our bleak little hut a cosy haven with the always-kept-burning stove. Beautiful though it was, there was no way we could make the Deanery cosy.

The Galley where we had our meals was in another building about 300 yards away and to get there we walked through the walled gardens of the Deanery which were beautifully tended by people, probably volunteers, who we never saw as we were out all day. Although the windows had compulsory blackout shutters which we were still supposed to close at night, we would sometimes leave them open during the summer months and just not put the lights on, go to bed in the dark and let the sun wake us in the mornings. One morning I woke about 6 a.m. and was alone, as the other two girls in my room were on leave. It was a beautiful June morning and as I glanced out of the window I was surprised to see what seemed to be an old man dressed rather strangely and poking a long stick into a huge bonfire in one of the wide herbaceous borders. My first thought was how strange to be having a bonfire in amongst the flowers in the middle of Summer. I turned away to start getting dressed and when I looked again, lo and behold, the man and his blazing fire had disappeared. As I was alone, I had no-one to tell what I had seen but decided that on my way across to the Galley for my breakfast I would have a good look at where the fire had appeared to be.

So it was a short while later that I stood in the garden, hardly able to grasp what I was seeing, or rather not seeing, because there were no signs at all that there had been a fire in the border. The flowers were all blooming or in bud and the elderly gardener was nowhere to be seen. I walked slowly on the way to get my breakfast and told one of the other Wrens there what I had seen and she said, 'Sounds like a ghost to me!'

Had I seen a ghost? Whatever it was, and whatever you want to think, I had definitely seen that old man and the fire which had so miraculously disappeared and the image has stayed with me ever since.

Work at Chatham was very similar to what we had done in Lowestoft except it was in airy offices above ground, so not so oppressive. One custom which was fiercely maintained at Chatham, as at sea, was the midday ration of a tot of rum. All Navy personnel working at the barracks were entitled to receive it so it was offered to us as we left after our morning work. Barby and I soon learned that if we didn't want our tot we were expected to take it and pass it on to one of the (mostly male) crew members waiting outside the gates who, having already had their own tot, would then knock ours back or pour it into a special flask for later!

We got to know about some courses that were being offered to help us find jobs when we were discharged from the service so I made enquiries and discovered there was a week-long course in Commercial Art to be held in Somerset and starting soon, which, even though I wasn't now thinking of going back to Art College or a future career in Fashion Design, I thought it would be a nice way to spend a week away from work doing something I enjoyed so I signed up for it.

There were about twelve of us on the course. Some had spent time at Art College like me and the rest, also like me, just wanted a week away from work. As it was a warm and sunny July, we spent time out in the countryside sketching and painting landscapes, then using them later to design adverts for some chosen well-known product. One day we visited a shoe factory and one evening our tutor had been given free tickets to an orchestral concert in Bath which we went along to, not sure if we'd like it but it was magical; the conductor was John Barbarolli who was very famous at the time and who invited us round back stage for a chat at the end – we thought that was pretty special. We were a jolly group and I really enjoyed the break and seeing more of the country. Since leaving Whitby, I had now spent time in London, Aberdeenshire, West Yorkshire, Norfolk, Kent, Cornwall and now Somerset – none of which I believe I would have been to if I hadn't joined the WRNS.

Back at the Barracks, Barby had been given a date for her discharge and I knew I would miss her, especially in the evenings and at weekends, so I really hoped I too would soon hear when I would become a civilian again. The weeks soon went by and Barby and I went shopping to spend the money she had been given, which we all got on leaving the service, to buy ourselves a 'civvy' outfit. We got to keep our uniforms but we hoped we wouldn't be wearing them ever again. Before I waved her off I asked her to let me know when she was going to marry Dan, her American fiancé, and she said she would and we made a pact that we would definitely arrange to meet up when we were both back in Yorkshire.

After Barby left I was sent to a place called Burghfield in Berkshire where I had to work in the Camp Sick Bay making beds, emptying bedpans, sweeping floors, stuff like that. Don't ask why I wasn't a Writer anymore – they just said I was coming up for discharge so had to do whatever needed doing and go wherever there was a shortfall, also that I would shortly go through my discharge routine from Burghfield. I was startled one day walking back to my quarters to literally bump into Tom, remember him? Mac's friend from when they were in Whitby and we hugged each other and he told me Mac and he had stayed together during the last of the North Africa campaign and that like himself Mac had survived. He didn't say any more and I didn't ask; we wished each other good luck and said 'cheerio,' and that was that. Obviously I was glad Mac was okay but I did feel strange for a good while after.

I had heard from home that my bother Peter was also in Berkshire studying and he managed to get in touch and arrange for us to meet, which one Saturday we did. It was good to get out of the campsite, see him again and chat about his new life and how he was adjusting to everything. We met in a café and had a proper 'Fry-up' – it was scrumptious! I told him I would soon be out of the WRNS and heading home and he said he would hope to be there too at Christmas. I felt a bit lost when he had gone. I seemed to be saying 'goodbye' a lot recently, sort of losing people and unsettled, a bit isolated. It didn't help when there was an outbreak of Dysentery in the camp so not only was the Sick Bay overcrowded, but I got the bug myself and as the Heads were quite a long walk outside from my sleeping quarters, it was no joke having to dash there several times during the night. I didn't get to know anyone very well at Burghfield, it being a kind of transit camp; most people seemed to be there one minute and gone the next so I was looking forward to news of leaving, of going home and moving on.

I don't think I was thinking too much about the future. I had been a Wren almost two years now and I had learnt a lot and although I knew I could cope with life on my own I still believed I could depend on my lovely parents to support me in whatever I decided to do and perhaps that I could help them in some way in the hotel, at least for a while. I was so looking forward to seeing how they had managed to get it open and running again and had no conception of how difficult it had been for them, as I said before, being so caught up in my own problems and difficulties; but I just knew then that I really wanted to be there, rather like the feeling I had had before leaving Broadings.

So it was that a few weeks later in September 1946 I was excitedly on my way back to Yorkshire, still in my uniform which had lost its stiffness and sort of bonded with me but which would soon no longer be part of my life. It was another goodbye.

Chapter 15

Everyone's Getting Married

WELL, THE HOTEL had managed to open for its first season for six years and I learnt that it had been more than just difficult. The pre-war staff members seemed to have more or less disappeared, married, moved away or whatever. My parents had tried to re-locate them all, including Chef Alf and Flo but without success. The first Chef they engaged had to be quickly disengaged as he kept turning up for duty very drunk! Also, it seemed that attitudes had changed and many young women were now less inclined to seek the kind of service work and low wages that they had been happy with before.

I imagine that Daddy would have had to obtain (or increase) a mortgage in order to try and restore and re-equip the place as the meagre amount of compensation would nowhere have covered that. Being an Accountant, he took care of that side of things and money was never discussed, like many other things then. I don't know whether even Mums knew how serious the financial situation was as she quickly just got on with managing the overall running, 'back of house', the catering and staff, etc.

So I turned up as that first season was almost over. It felt strange getting used to it all again, especially without the old 'crew'. The old camaraderie seemed to be gone and there seemed to be repeated arguments and what seemed like jealousies going on which Mums kept having to sort out. It seemed strange in a way that although the new staff were getting more money than the pre-war ones, they seemed less happy.

I had a bedroom on the top floor until the hotel closed down in October when, like before the war, I would move down to one on the first floor. I started to help Daddy in the office, mostly with typing and sorting out the post. Midge was home from her time in the WAAF and had become engaged to an airman she had met called Len. Bets had also been de-mobbed and had a job at the BBC in London as a secretary. I haven't yet told you this, but Bets had always really liked 'young' Eric (you remember, son of father Eric) and as he was now out of the Navy and working locally, she travelled up to Whitby to see him whenever she could. I guess Eric liked her too because just before Christmas they got engaged. Maureen, my friend from school who wasn't even 18 yet, had met and become engaged to Johnny who had been away in the forces and was seven years older than Mo which was lovely; but I had the feeling I was getting left behind as I didn't even have a regular boyfriend – well, I didn't have an irregular one either, did I? (Unless you count Tony and that wouldn't be right.)

I took stock of myself. I had always thought of myself as reasonable-looking and tried to make the best of what I was born with whilst wishing I was taller, had longer legs, curlier hair, a different mouth, etc., etc., etc. Anyway, I was stuck with being 5ft 2' with grey eyes and longish brown hair which I now trained to curl under in what we called a Pageboy Bob, and which I tried to make as much like the hairstyle of an American film star at the time called Rita Hayworth. Figuratively speaking, I was okay – my figure, I mean! It was slim now it had recovered from those first few months in the WRNS, and I suppose my dancing had helped. I remember once when I was very young asking Daddy, 'What do you have to do to be beautiful?' – and he said something like, 'Well, it's important to be beautiful on the inside, or you can't be really beautiful on the outside, even if you are' – which I sort of understood. Anyway in that year of Our Lord 1946 I decided I would do my best to be attractive on the inside whilst making the best of what I had on the outside, and, I thought, that would surely help me get through life, and maybe even find me a soulmate to share it with.

I'm not very comfortable telling you about me, which is different from telling you about my life and as you may have noticed, I haven't even told you my name, have I? I just thought it was probably time that you had some idea of the sort of person I had become, outside and inside, that's if you're still interested. Personality-wise I know I did pretend to be more confident than I felt but I became quite good at bluffing my way through uncomfortable or difficult situations which didn't of course always work. I was quite a 'people-pleaser' because I wanted to be liked and really hated being challenged, criticised or put on the spot, so to speak – yeah, you've guessed it, over sensitive and quite easily hurt, but I wouldn't tell you, I would run away and cry in private. Although I knew I had a good sense of humour and loved to laugh, I was and still am rubbish at telling jokes and leave that to those who can. I'm curious about stuff because, as you know I often failed to pay enough attention at school so needed to catch up on a lot of things. I do respect and admire those who have studied hard and contribute a lot to society and always hoped to be useful in some way, and at very least responsible for myself and supportive of others. I believed in a spiritual God who though I didn't fully understand was a non-controlling power for good as opposed to the Devil who is a controlling power for all things negative and bad. Of course I had my dreams of romance and a 'Mr Right' to love and share my life with and did quite often fear that it may never happen. Well folks, this is as I remember myself at age 20. Needless to say I've changed a bit and moved on somewhat since then as life tends to help us to do, doesn't it? Anyway, that's more than enough of me for now, or even then!

I got in touch with Barby and invited her over to stay and she came on the train the following week. It was great to see her again and go over how we were both getting on in civilian life. I was sad to hear she had broken off her engagement to Dan, her American G.I. She said the fact that he had now gone back to America and the disapproval from her Father had proved too much. I felt really worried for Barby somehow, that she had missed out on her personal happiness and made a wrong decision to please her Father, but she seemed to be okay with it. I had a fun time showing Barby around the town and all my favourite places. We went to 'the pictures' and saw 'The Red Shoes' starring the ballerina Moira Shearer which we both thought was magical and also one with Fred Astaire and Ginger Rogers – I think it was 'Swingtime' which was so romantic and made me long to dance again.

Barby's visit had been great but when she had gone I began to think about getting some training for something more interesting than secretarial work and found an advert in the newspaper for a place in London offering a course in Beauty Culture which didn't seem too expensive so I talked to Mums and Daddy about it. As always they were enthusiastic about me branching out into what was then a fairly new occupation and Mums said I could probably stay with Nan and Bert, our relations in London. So I wrote off about it and in just a few weeks found myself at the Mary Wood School of Beauty in Knightsbridge, London. The course was for three weeks and I enjoyed learning about facial massage, make-up and manicure, etc. I also enjoyed spending time with my Aunt and Uncle – they lived in a really nice house in Surrey and I caught the train up to the city every week-day with Bets – and finding my way around war-torn London was an experience in itself. Harry was there and looked fine apart from being very thin but I discovered that ever since returning home from the prisoner of war camp where he had been for five years, he kept (as I think I told you earlier) washing his hands all the time and as yet seemed to have no ideas about a career or work or to train for anything. Obviously, his parents were just glad to have him home safe and were not inclined to push him into anything.

After the course and a taste of London, it was good to be back home in Whitby bumping into old friends in town and catching up on each other's lives. All the barbed wire had gone from the cliff top but large areas of the moors were still bare of heather since the tank training had churned it all up. The Spa was struggling to get back to its former glory, and Frank Gomez hadn't returned to lead the orchestra so there was no sign of my acting/dancing/singing friend Rozzy. As there was no Beauty Salon in the town, there wasn't anywhere I could apply for a job and it was looking like the only way to get work and gain some experience was going to be over in Scarborough again. Maybe it would have been a good idea to think of that before going on the course. However as luck would have it my parents were friendly with a lady called Dorothy something-or-other who owned a Hairdressing Salon in Whitby and who had been thinking of providing a facial and manicure service as well so when she learnt I had been on the 'beautification course' she was happy to take me on. Well, I had my first peacetime job and a salary of £2 a week; yes, I know it seems small compared to the inflated wages of today but it was a lot more than I had been getting as a Wren and it made sense to use the training and the money spent on it.

There were two hairdressers at the salon. The older one, Phyllis, didn't take kindly to me at first as she had been expecting to be sent on a course of Beauty Culture in London herself which the owner cancelled when she took me on, possibly pleased that she wouldn't have to fork out for it. After a while, they both accepted me into the fold but business for my services was very slow and most days I ended up sweeping the floor after haircuts, manning or I suppose woman-ing the reception and tidying the salon at closing time. After the war years of austerity most women were not used to indulging in such things as a face massage or a manicure, especially in a small town like Whitby, so the fact that it was available hadn't really sunk in and would seem like an unnecessary extravagance. However, after about a month and some advertising in the local paper I had three regular clients for facials and quite a few manicures; but it was hardly enough to pay my wages and eventually Dorothy, the lady boss, and I decided it was probably too soon to expect much more and after a few months we called it a day.

It was almost Christmas. Mums had been busy producing the autumn play for the Am Drams – I think it was a mystery by Agatha Christie – and Daddy had had a small part in it. The plays were always well supported and well received. During the war, the plays and the Society had been suspended but some members, including Mums, had at some point agreed to join with the Army in providing entertainment for service people stationed locally. Mums told me that it had been very helpful as the officer in charge of putting the shows together was a theatre director in civilian life and had taught them a great deal. Sam, who had been producing before the war, had stepped down from the job and urged Mums to take over, which she had bravely done. The Dramatic Society historically produced two plays a year, in Autumn and early Spring, allowing about six weeks for rehearsals, etc., so Vee, my Mums, was already thinking about plans for the next production which was to be *Flare Path*, a story about life in the RAF during the war.

Like most small town Am Dram Societies, ours was usually short of young people, especially young male members with the time or inclination to put themselves in the spotlight, as it were; so as *Flare Path* had a mostly young cast Mums was on the lookout for likely candidates to join and audition for the play early in the new year. There were plenty of young men and women who had returned home from being in the forces, but they were mostly busy re-establishing themselves in work, or getting married or just not interested. However, there was a new young dentist in town who Daddy had met at his men's club and had invited round to meet Mums and me. He was called Gordon, had spent the war years in the RAF and had married his wife, Bobbie, a WAAF whilst they were both still serving; they had a little 3-year-old girl called Susan and Bobbie was pregnant again.

Needless to say Mums went to work on persuading Gordon to join the WADS and audition for the lead in *Flare Path* as she could see straight away he had the looks and potential for the part and after all he had served in the RAF; but he proved very resistant, never having had the slightest desire to perform anything anywhere. But Mums didn't give up easily and eventually won him over by pointing out the benefits of getting involved locally and meeting a variety of local people which would not only be good socially but would offer the possibility of more patients in his dental practice. Well, that must have done it! After Christmas, Gordon bravely took on the lead roll in *Flare Path* and turned out to be a 'natural'; Bobbie gave birth to their son, Peter, and they became our good family friends.

However, we're still in 1946 and Tony telephoned. He was out of the Service and home with his parents in Chester. He invited me over to stay the following weekend and I had no reason not to accept. His parents and older brother were really nice – they made me feel very welcome and said Tony had told them a lot about me which made me wonder 'what could he have told them about me?' (Well, you do think that when people say that, don't you?) On Saturday evening we went out for dinner to a lovely restaurant and on Sunday, after lunch, Tony drove the two of us in his parent's car around the lovely Cheshire countryside. He told me he was applying to university to study medicine and I said I would be staying at home to support my parents for the time being. It was a lovely pleasant time, but there was still no obvious chemistry between us which we both just seemed to accept. I did think it would be nice to have Tony over to stay with us over Christmas and he agreed to come for Boxing Day. I told him it would coincide with us going to the Golf Dance so to bring his dinner suit or else his uniform which would be okay. We said our goodbyes knowing we would soon be seeing each other; we were as I keep saying, good friends, but I couldn't help thinking on the train home that the time was coming when the platonic nature of our friendship must surely come up.

My parents and some friends had arranged a weekend in London just for a break and some theatre and shopping and said I was to go too. We went by train and stayed at the Cumberland Hotel at the top of Oxford Street. It was a new experience for me and I really enjoyed going to the two shows we chose, the acting, the atmosphere, ice cream in the interval or drinks if you wanted to join the scrum at the bar. With the Christmas dances looming, Mums bought me my first long dress during a visit to Harrods. It was a pink off-the-shoulder creation with a push-up bra (!) to go with it. After one show, an American Musical, I think it was *Guys and Dolls*, which incidentally, for some reason Daddy hated, we went to a nightclub which was underground in Berkeley Square. There were eight of us, my parents, Auntie Doff, Madge and Eric, Bert and Nan (who came to join us from the suburbs) and me. There was a small band playing very slow romantic tunes, couples dancing close together, the lights were low and the atmosphere seductive; I don't know how Auntie Doff felt, being there like me without a partner, but I found myself feeling very out of place and having to pretend I was enjoying myself when I wasn't.

Nightclubs then hadn't progressed, if that's the right word, into the Disco clubs of today where you can dance to your heart's content without a partner and lose your inhibitions, and often your intentions and have lots of noisy fun; yet in spite of my situation and a sort of 'left out' feelings at that time, I remember the effect it had on me and hope there are still a few nightclubs like that one in Berkeley Square in 1946, and still people who are lucky enough to fall in love in that dreamy atmosphere as I would have loved to do. Back at the Hotel, I looked out of the window of my room onto the London streets and had some strange feelings; I was being treated by my lovely parents to a really nice weekend break and a change from the dreary wartime years, and although I was enjoying most of it, I longed to be with someone my own age. I wasn't a teenager anymore – I was nearly 21 and felt I was missing out somehow.

Chapter 16

Lost and Found

BACK IN WHITBY there was a lot going on one way and another. Maureen and Johnny had planned their wedding for the following August and Mo had asked me to be her chief bridesmaid along with ex-school friends Doreen and Marian and Johnny's two little nieces who were aged about 7 and 5. It was to be quite a grand affair and I was excited to be going to be part of it, dressing up after all the years of austerity, lots of people, friends coming together for a happy occasion. Also, Eric and Bets were planning their wedding for the following December and Bets asked Midge and me to be her bridesmaids.

Christmas arrived at last and at the Hospital Ball, we actually organised a 'young table', as opposed to sitting with our parents! which consisted of Bets and Eric, Midge and her fiancé Len, Pym (another ex-school friend) and Ian her husband, me and Colin, who I had dated a couple of times; sorry, I didn't tell you about him, he was one of our group but it was one of those things where he wanted us to be more than platonic friends and I didn't. Anyway, finally I was at a Christmas dance with people my own age and it was great.

Stylish, even glamorous things were beginning to be back in the shops and I had some lovely presents that year. The atmosphere was so much more relaxed and light hearted. Tony duly arrived on Boxing Day and we sort of rushed around getting ourselves 'dolled up' for the Golf Dance where we had arranged for another 'young table'. Everyone immediately took to Tony who had the knack of fitting in and joining in whoever he was with. I wore my lovely pink dress with its push-up bra and it was another fun evening. My parents too loved Tony and secretly, I think, thought he and I were an 'item' which of course, as you now know, we strangely weren't. Anyway the few days passed happily and Tony was gone once more without any 'snogging' or talking about it or, well, lack of it.

During the traditional 'first-footing' of New Year's Eve I bumped into Paul somewhere along the way and he sort of pulled me aside and asked if I would meet him somewhere soon. I was a bit taken aback as I thought he was completely 'over' me but as I still did have feelings for him I said I would, and we arranged to meet and have a walk on the beach. For the next few days I felt really hopeful in a way about the possibility of another chance for Paul and me and went off to meet him in a happy mood. We set off down the zig-zag path to the beach, holding hands and running most of the way, then strolling along the sea wall above the sands and eventually sitting on some rocks at the far end. All of a sudden, he grabbed me rather roughly and before I could say anything I was being pushed over on the rocks feeling overwhelmed and very uncomfortable and struggling to pull myself up and away from him.

'What are you doing for heavens' sake?' I shouted.

'What's the matter with you?' he sort of growled.

This just wasn't the Paul I knew and even though I obviously understood what he was trying to do, it didn't feel either the time or the place to be trying to do it and somehow, in an instant any romantic and I suppose naive idea I had had about his invitation was gone. Maybe my reaction was prudish and I had ended up hurting him again, but I'm afraid after a bit more wrestling and a few harsh words we both had to accept that the episode was a disaster and once again had to go our separate ways, which we did.

I really wasn't doing very well in the love life department, and another strange incident didn't exactly help me feel any better.

I've mentioned our family friends Reg and Win, Midge's parents; well, Reg had a brother called Jimmy, quite a character who had had a brief spell as an actor in London but who now helped out in the family bakery business and was active in the WADS, usually in the make-up department and was also inclined to do a bit of matchmaking. A new young locum doctor called Dan Something-or-other had recently joined a local practice and Jimmy must at some point have decided he and I should, (sorry) would meet. Well, we didn't actually meet but this Dan telephoned me one day, introduced himself and asked me out to dinner at a recently opened Country Club on the edge of town. Well, I thought 'why not'? I'd recently managed to acquire a rather super bronzy-coloured skirt with a wide waistband and an almost off the shoulder top which I felt really good in and decided would be perfect for my blind 'date'.

Well, it all seemed very exciting. I hadn't even met this guy but had heard (Whitby gossip) that he was sort of sophisticated and rather good-looking and my friends seemed to think we would hit it off. Well, the evening arrived and lo and behold Doctor Dan arrived to pick me up in a very racy-looking sports car (please don't ask me what the make was) and certainly did look a bit racy himself and older than I thought – maybe he had finished his medical degree after war service or something; anyway, off we went.

Well, that I'm afraid is the end of the exciting bit because when we arrived at the restaurant, Jimmy was there waiting for us, supposedly to do the introductions but which had obviously already been done. Dan went to the bar to order pre-dinner drinks and Jimmy, who stayed with us and me, sat down at a table and chatted away and chatted away and er, chatted away some more and then I noticed that after bringing our drinks, Dan had returned to the bar and was engaged in what looked like a very intimate conversation with the bar lady (who was, admittedly, very attractive). Anyway, eventually we had dinner: very nice, Jimmy with us, polite conversation, after which our host quickly paid the bill and acted like he couldn't wait to drive me back home. I thanked him for the meal and leaned over to give him a kiss, (please don't ask why I did that) and that was it. I had the distinct feeling, well, thought, that he couldn't wait to drive his racy car straight back to the restaurant to continue intimate chatting and 'whatever' with attractive bar lady – so, what was that all about? Why on earth had he asked me? Or Jimmy, for that matter? Boyfriend-less I may be but I sure wasn't desperate enough for racy, confusing, bar lady desiring, Doctor Dan.

Well, preparations were well underway for the start of the second post-war season of the hotel and whilst Daddy coped with, and worried about bookings and rebuilding the good reputation they had gained pre-war, Mums was embroiled in producing *Flare Path*, the rehearsals of which had all been carried out in the hotel dining room, and there was the usual meetings about the set, its furnishings and who and from where they could borrow this and that plus transport, lighting, advertising, etc. One member, our local Optician called Hugh, was also a keen photographer, very artistic and a wizard at designing the sets and with the co-operation of local supporters, whether members or not, the sets were always so much more than just 'amateur adequate' and received great applause as the curtain went up. Reg was often a reliable cast member as was Auntie Doff, and Win was always the very efficient and trusted prompt.

Back to the hotel, I had started to help Daddy in the office, my Writer training coming in handy and although he had always coped on his own, he seemed to be glad I was there and

I noticed how distracted he sometimes seemed to be and worried, of course that enquiries and bookings were not as good as before the war. One of the reasons obviously was that many holiday-makers who previously were happy with a bucket and spade and a sometimes rain-soaked British seaside break were now being lured to the fast-growing overseas resorts and the more reliable sunshine of southern Spain and other Mediterranean hot-spots. Daddy had applied for a residential licence for serving alcohol on the premises but it had been refused, don't ask me why please! Anyway, we had to deal with what we had and I was aware it was going to be more of a struggle than in the past and that it was all causing my Daddy more than the pain in his leg, which incidentally also seemed to be worse and bothering him more.

I had persuaded my parents to let me set up a small beauty salon on the top floor and had cards printed to place in each bedroom that facials and manicures were available and had equipped myself with the creams and other products from my training source in London, Mary Wood. Quite soon, although the residents didn't seem very responsive, I started to get some regular local clients and although this was encouraging, it only served to allow me to afford to keep buying the products. I had a lot to learn about business and costing, but at least I was getting some experience. We used to laugh that, having no lift, by the time I had led a client up the several flights of stairs to the top floor, they would be in desperate need of my services!

As far as I can remember, the charge per person for a week's stay at the hotel in 1947 inclusive of all meals plus afternoon tea was ten guineas (ten pounds, ten shillings, or £10.50p). One day just before Easter, I was in the office with Daddy when a youngish man came in and walked up to the reception window and enquired how much for one person for the Easter week (fees remained the same at holiday times), so

Daddy gave him a brochure and told him the cost whereupon he turned and strode towards the door, looked back at Daddy and said:

'I wanted to stay here, not buy the place.'

Of course we were taken aback and tried to laugh about it, knowing that our prices were completely fair and very good value compared with similar establishments and the cost of living at that time, but it was an unpleasant thing to happen after the struggle to get going again and deep down I think it added to Daddy's worries. Even though I realised that the man was obviously out of touch, rude and not worth being bothered about, it nevertheless upset me.

In May I was 21 and Mums organised a sort of party for me in the Annex which had been built on to the Dining Room about two years before the war. Strangely I don't remember much about it; there was a very nice buffet and a cake and a few local friends came. For some reason Daddy wasn't there or my brother who was now working for a large firm of Opticians in Reading. Mums kept popping in to see if we were okay and we played a few games and that was about it – not really much more to say about it.

I had invited Barby to my 21st and although she didn't come, she phoned and asked me to go and stay the following weekend in Bradford. She had a new boyfriend called Brian and she said on the Saturday night we would be going to a rugby dance after the game and that a friend of Brian's who was called Peter would be my blind date. She said I was to bring my prettiest dress as Peter was really nice and had eyelashes that would sweep the floor. Well as you know by now my recent luck with dates, blind or otherwise, had been a bit of a disaster; but I was looking forward to the break and seeing my friend again and the rugby dance sounded fun.

I borrowed a rather sophisticated blue dress from Mums – it was lucky we were about the same size – and packed my one and only pair of high-heeled shoes and precious (tan) nylon stockings, before happily setting off for Bradford. My hair was okay by then because I faithfully brushed it 100 times every night so it was quite shiny and long and, oh yes, I popped the push-up bra in the case as well.

Barby was really bubbly and seemed to be enjoying life and we had fun getting ready for our night out. Her Mum seemed very sweet-natured but rather nervous and I could understand how, when I met her father as he rather dominated all conversation, he had probably been the main cause of Barby breaking off her engagement to her Dan. Anyway moving on, the plan for the evening was that Brian would pick us up in his jalopy of a car and we would then drive to Ilkley to meet Peter in the downstairs bar of the Middleton Hotel. Brian and Peter had both played rugby for their team in the afternoon.

I suppose I was apprehensive about meeting my blind date and his sweep-the-floor eyelashes but decided it wasn't the end of the world if we didn't like each other and I would do my best to enjoy the evening anyway; maybe we could even laugh about it which, as it happened, we did.

The Middleton is, or rather was, a large, very nice hotel in the middle of Ilkley which is in the heart of the Yorkshire Dales and a very popular landmark of the area. The downstairs public bar was crowded, mostly young people off to a dance somewhere as were we. As we edged our way in I became aware that Brian was waving to someone getting drinks up at the bar and as we edged and shuffled forward, suddenly there in front of me were the eyelashes, the blue eyes, the blond hair and the person I had almost been dreading meeting who was smiling at me and I thought was, well, absolutely gorgeous.

After hasty, rather muddled introductions we had our drinks, beers for them, shandies for us and piled into the car once more to head for Skipton where our dance was probably by now in full swing. There was lots of cheeky chat on the drive there, lots of laughs and I thought well, so far, so good, as it were.

The dance was at a pub which had a large function room/dance floor but much to my dismay there seemed to be more drinking than dancing going on as Brian and Peter had met up with lots of their Rugby mates all celebrating having won their last game of the season in the afternoon and I learnt Peter had scored a couple of tries so everyone was patting him on the back. Well somehow, we all got separated and I'm not sure how, but I found myself with a group of celebrating strangers who sort of took me into their circle and kept insisting I had more to drink (I think it was whisky) and then bought me another, which stupidly I had, trying to be one of them and accepted by them I suppose. Well it wasn't very long before I had an overwhelming desire to be sick! Desperate to find Barby, I managed to extricate myself from the boozy group and get to where I might find her. Then, thankfully, I saw Peter and pleaded with him to show me the way to the rest room. Well, he could see I was in trouble I suppose, and instead he put his arm around me and took me outside into the fresh air and kept saying how sorry he was to have abandoned me whereupon as we walked along the street I very suddenly threw up – all three whiskies plus the shandy from the Middleton and all over someone's bright red car! Peter gave me his hanky (men usually had one then) to mop my face and we stayed where we were until I felt better. I told him I wasn't used to drinking much at all and hadn't had much to eat, but understanding and kind as he was I felt pretty sure this would be our last, as well as our first meeting and was fed up with myself for messing things up. He took the hanky away from me and chucked it in a nearby rubbish bin.

Peter smoked – almost everyone did then – and he lit up a cigarette as we leaned against the red car in the moonlight which didn't seem very romantic then but now I think about it, it sort of was. He didn't seem anxious to go back into the pub and we talked for a while about this and that and he said he had thought I was going to be really ugly because Barby was so attractive and I laughed and said he wasn't wrong then and that I had been pretty sure we wouldn't like each other. Then it struck me that in spite of having left me at the mercy of the folk inside to start with, when faced with my unpleasant situation he had stayed with me, and didn't seem to be completely put off by this wimpy girl who had thrown up almost all over him. After a while we went back inside but just before we did, he suddenly pulled me close to him and kissed me. Wow, I was lost!

Chapter 17

Lots of Feelings

BACK IN THE NOISE and smoke-filled fog of the pub I headed for the Girls Room where I washed my face and tried to refurbish it with some make-up and put a comb through my hair, not exactly how I'd started out but it would have to do; then it was out to face the rest of the evening as best I could and definitely without alcohol. I could see Peter talking to someone; this was his home territory so he would know most of the people there. Then I caught his eye and he came over and put his arm round me and asked if I was okay. We found Barby and Brian and spent the rest of the evening together or on the dance floor. They hadn't realised Peter and I had been apart and Peter had thought I was with them; anyway whatever had happened it seemed to be okay in the end and eventually we piled back into Brian's car and headed back to Bradford dropping Peter off in Ilkley where he lived with his Mum.

Barby and I talked way into the small hours. She said she liked Brian a lot but didn't think it was forever and I told her I was a bit starry- eyed about Peter and hoped I'd get to see him again.

The next day, Sunday, Brian had arranged for us to go with him to see his younger brother at his boarding school and take him out for lunch. After breakfast there was a phone call from Brian to say he had asked Peter to come too; they had both been to the school which is called Giggleswick and lies in the heart of the Yorkshire Dales, so it would be a lovely drive over there; but as you can guess I was really happy as it meant I would see Peter again.

In Ilkley we stopped to pick him up and when he climbed into the back of the car next to me, he straight away took hold of my hand and he kept looking at me and smiling and whispered something in my ear, something funny, I can't remember what it was but it was just for us. I was sort of swooning inside.

It was a lovely day and after we had given Brian's brother, Tom, his treat and delivered him safely back to school, we stopped on the way back and walked for a while on the hillside and sat on a craggy dry-stone wall gazing out over the miles and miles of open, unspoilt moorland and not needing to say much at all.

Before leaving us again, Peter asked me for my home telephone number and I told him that if he liked he could come over and stay with us some weekend. I had discovered he was an Engineering graduate and worked in his family firm of Gas Engineers in Keighley. He was 22, years old and apart from work and rugby he also liked to play golf so I couldn't really see much chance of him getting over to Whitby soon or very often. My heart sank a bit as we said goodbye.

That evening Barby and I were dressing up again as her father had arranged for us to go out for a meal with a client of his from Norway who was over on a business visit. For some reason her Mum didn't come so there was just the four of us and we were to meet at the Middleton in Ilkley once more. Sven was a typical tall, blond, blue-eyed Norwegian who spoke perfect English and we were soon seated and chatting away in the upstairs restaurant which had a small dance floor. While we were waiting for our food to arrive, Sven asked me to dance and as we were rather slowly gliding around the floor lo and behold who did I spy out of the corner of my eye but Peter, sitting at a table with an older couple who turned out to be his mother and step-father. I smiled and waved to him and he waved back but it was a strange moment.

I desperately wanted to explain to him that Sven wasn't anyone to do with me and that he had a wife back in Norway but obviously that wasn't possible. After a while Peter did come over to our table and say hello but it still felt, well, awkward somehow.

The next day I went home after what had been a pretty eventful time whichever way you look at it. I did talk a lot about a young man I had met called Peter and I don't think my parents were left in any doubt about the fact that I liked him... a lot.

It was a tough few days before he called. Would he? Maybe he had just been polite? Had I just imagined that he felt the same as me? Well, nothing is certain, is it? Look at my record – at sixteen I had been in love and thought myself the luckiest girl in the world and lost it. At eighteen I was sure I was in love and you know what happened there! Then there was a sort of uncertain 'how to love' Tony and we won't even mention Doctor Dan!

Well, okay, I know, by today's standards you would say 'I could have called him' – but oh no, no, no, not then! That way you wouldn't know whether he was really interested or not. No, you just had to wait. If 'he' didn't call, then at least you knew where you stood and could deal with it. Nowadays, well, I think, it's all got a bit too easy to, well, perhaps 'get it wrong'.

Before the end of the week, I think it was Thursday, he called! I loved his voice and the very slight hint of West Yorkshire in it. He said he'd like to come over and visit the following weekend if that was okay and could he bring a friend? Well I knew we still had spare rooms so of course it was alright, of course, of course of course! I said, 'Yes, of course it's alright!' – my heart was singing. Well, it felt as if it was.

It was June now and the season in full swing and even though the hotel wasn't full, there was plenty for me to do to help out, either in the office, shopping, or attending to an occasional client in my beauty room. Daddy's leg was worse, and he now had to use a calliper which is a type of splint with a padded top; you sit in and it takes the weight of the bad leg. Then he used a crutch as well so it was difficult for him to get around and he needed me.

I had become friendly with Bobbie, Gordon's wife, and would sometimes 'baby sit' for them to go out; also, she and I would go to the 'pictures' about once a week when Gordon would stay with their kids. The social life of the town, among our group of friends anyway, had changed in some ways since the war; instead of meeting at the Spa, which was still struggling to be revived, it was more likely to be at the Golf Club or one of the recently refurbished town or village pubs. One such pub was The Beehive Inn in Newholm which had become very popular and the place 'to be', especially for some reason, late on Sunday mornings, before lunch, or after church.

Our relatives from London came to visit and stayed at the hotel instead of with Aunt Sally at Havelock Place. Uncle Bert had acquired a very smart Jaguar car and persuaded us to go to the Beehive for a drink before the hotel's busy lunchtime. Mums went in the new posh car but Daddy said he would go independently in 'Jo' and I went with him. When it was time to drive back Uncle Bert asked me, 'didn't I want a spin in his new car then?'

Daddy had already got himself and his crutches into 'Jo' so, to my everlasting shame, I said did he mind if I went back with the others and of course he said 'no'. Well 'Jo' was ahead of us all the way and when we reached the hotel, as the Jag swept into the front area and Daddy turned into the rear driveway, I just somehow felt terrible – it was as if I had chosen a seemingly successful uncle over my seemingly failing father and a posh Jag over our beloved Jo and no amount of saying sorry now was going to change that. If only I could run that scene again, I would say 'no way' to my uncle, jump into 'Jo' beside my Daddy and wave both my arms in the air as we swept into the drive ahead of him; but I hadn't done that and I hated myself.

Maureen's wedding was to be in August and one day the other bridesmaids and me all gathered at her Mum's shop to decide on our dresses and to be fitted. We ended up with blue taffeta and lots of laughing over choosing what to put on our heads. It was a long way from making do with so little during the war or me being pinned into someone else's dress in Cornwall.

Then it was Saturday and Peter arrived with his friend Robbie in Robbie's sports car, which I suppose was one reason he had asked if it was okay for him to come too. Anyway, when I introduced them to my parents, they were confused as to which one was the one I had been going on about which was a bit awkward until I sorted it out and put them straight: 'For heaven's sake it's Peter, the blond one. Robbie's the dark one and I've only just met him myself!'

I showed them to their rooms. Each had a single on the first floor and when we were alone Peter and I kissed and said how much we had wanted to meet again. We decided we'd drive over to Scarborough that evening and go to a dance at one of the hotels there, and that we'd have to find a partner for Robbie. Well, most of my friends were already hooked up, engaged or married so I had to put my thinking cap on and eventually contacted Heather, who was actually a friend of a friend and someone I didn't really know very well but who agreed to come along.

After we had some lunch, I showed the boys around town and along the beach and we chucked a ball about, and ran around and laughed a lot before scrambling back up the cliff to the hotel for tea. Then it was time to tart up for our trip to Scarborough.

Obviously, Robbie was driving so Peter and I squashed into the back seat leaving room for Heather next to him. Robbie got out and opened the door for her as we introduced them and in she got and off we went along the winding road to Scarborough singing 'Whip Crack Away, Whip Crack Away' from the musical 'Calamity Jane' as loud as we could and I hadn't been so happy for ages.

We went to The Crown Hotel where there was a dance on and it was a really fun evening. There was a live band and lots of people all dressed up which seemed really glamorous, sort of like a Fred Astaire film and the four of us really seeming to enjoy each other's company. Peter's dancing, Robbie's too, was mostly confined to the slow 'hold you close and shuffle' type, but even though, as you know, I loved to quick-step and jive, slow and close with Peter at that moment in time was just fine thank you very much. On the drive back we were much quieter and Robbie dropped Peter and me off at the Hotel before taking Heather home. It was well after midnight so everyone seemed to have gone to bed as we crept quietly in through the front hall where the night porter John was waiting to lock up. Needless to say Daddy was still up wanting to know we were safely back.

I went with Peter to his room on the way to mine, yes of course we got close and kissed a lot but as I've already told you, but somehow feel I have to tell you again, we just didn't go any further – it was a kind of innocence and I suppose ignorance, even fear, that kept us 'on the edge'. I didn't know what experience Peter had, I just know that in the spirit of that time, he respected my belief or whatever you like to call it and when we finally said 'goodnight' and I left him, it didn't feel at all like a rejection of anything, but like the beginning of something very special.

Next morning I joined the boys for breakfast in the residents' dining room which was weird in a way, being 'waited on' by those who were also my friends, and being a guest in my own home. Afterwards we drove up to the golf club and played nine holes – well, *they* played nine holes, I was well out of practice and just tried to keep up. Afterwards we joined up with a few of my friends in the clubhouse before getting back to the hotel in time for lunch. Peter tried to grill Robbie as to his feelings about his date with Heather, but all he would say was 'very nice', or 'okay' so we sort of gave up on that, but afterwards, I found out that although she had seemed to be happy enough at the time, Heather hadn't taken to Robbie at all. Well, that's life, as they say, and I had been in that situation before, remember, with Tom and lovely Mara. Oh well, so be it.

I kissed Peter goodbye that evening and as I waved them off, I didn't want him to be gone. We had talked a lot when we were alone and it seemed like we felt the same about a lot of things and I felt safe with him and comfortable and best of all he made me laugh. I felt I couldn't wait for the next time we would be together.

Chapter 18

Insecurity – Me?

I HAD BEEN on the phone to Barby, to tell her about Peter and Robbie's visit and she asked me to her 21st 'do' which was in a couple of weeks and was to be at the Middleton Hotel once more. She said, 'Don't worry, Peter will definitely be invited!' So of course I was happy – there would be another chance for us to see each other and I couldn't wait.

I did as much as I could to help Daddy before buzzing off to Bradford once more on the train. In spite of my spins round the Rattray airfield, I hadn't yet had any proper driving lessons or applied for a test and even if I had, I wouldn't have been able to borrow 'Jo' to drive over as Daddy needed it. Hardly any of my friends drove; if they did, they would have to borrow the family car, that's if they had one, but mostly we walked everywhere locally, and for long trips it was the train or bus.

I had to borrow another dress of Mum's for Barby's 'do' I thought the pink one was too ball-dressy for a 21st. I was really enjoying my much improved social life and what I liked to think of as my new love life. As it was Barby's party, we were there early for her to greet all her guests and when I spied Peter he was, like all the men, in a dinner jacket and looked absolutely gorgeous. Needless to say, everyone was bringing a gift so it became my job to look after them all and find a place to keep them for her to open later.

There was a buffet and then dancing in the upstairs dining area where we had been that night with Sven. I had by now talked to Peter about that and he said he had wondered if I was hooked up with him so maybe it hadn't been such a bad coincidence after all? There was dancing and a buffet, Barby was 'bumped' 21 times and toasted and we all sang 'For She's a Jolly Good Fellow' and that was that. A few of her closest friends including Peter were asked back to the house for a 'night cap' or a hot drink. Barby opened her pressies and then, when we were all sitting around talking and joking, I looked across the room to see that the girl sitting next to Peter was leaning up close to him and they were holding hands in an intimate sort of way. I was shocked, puzzled I suppose, and, stupid though it may sound, I didn't want to stay and see them like that. I got up and shot out of the room and up to the bathroom where I sat on the edge of the bath and buried my face in a towel. Stupid or not, I felt as if my lovely new world was once more falling apart.

There was a knock at the door and I thought it might be Barby, worried about me rushing off like that, but it was Peter. He did look a bit sheepish and he locked the door behind him and put his arms round me and said he had known the girl, who was called Denise, for a long time and that she tended to flirt with all the boys and it meant nothing.

I felt a bit of an idiot, and became aware of how I had started to take it for granted that we were a couple when actually we hadn't known each other very long and were still very young and that Peter had every right to see other girls if he chose to; anyway, I had now let him know, hadn't I, how strongly I felt about us, well *him*, and I suppose I had also shown him how insecure I was.

Later when they had all gone and Barby and I were talking, I told her about it and how jealous I had felt and how stupid. She said she was pretty sure Peter liked me a lot and the fact that he had come up after me was a good sign and anyway, she said, look on the bright side, he was definitely single and had already shown he was keen to keep seeing me.

My doubts and fears were all put to rest the next day when just before I left to catch the bus home, there was a phone call for me from the man himself saying he hoped to get over to Whitby to see me again soon, if that was okay. That was definitely okay but I had learnt not to take things for granted and not to let my dreams and feelings run away with me.

The summer was jogging along quite well, and Maureen and Johnny's wedding was to be a big event. Mo had asked me to do her make-up before we all got ready at her house, and she looked lovely. Church Square was crowded with onlookers and our bridesmaid's car had difficulty making its way to the main door of the Church. The reception was at the Metropole Hotel which only a couple of years before had been full of Army personnel and hit by a stray bomb. It was now fully restored to its pre-war grandness and we all enjoyed being part of what was a rather grand occasion. Maureen was only 18 and it seemed such a short time since we had coped together at St Mary's School. She had left soon after I had and spent two years at the Grammar, becoming head girl and attaining her Higher School Cert. I couldn't help feeling that she could have continued on to academic and career success at anything she chose but she had chosen Johnny and marriage. I was very fond of my friend Mo and could only hope and wish for her happiness. I knew she would probably continue to help her Mum in the dress shop, which she did.

The next time Peter came over it was in Brian's car with Barby and the four of us had a really fun weekend. We spent time relaxing on the beach, Scarborough again to a dance on Saturday night and up to The Beehive on Sunday, meeting up with my local friends who were usually all there. It may seem strange now, but drinking wasn't really a big part of going to the pub; the boys would seem to enjoy a pint or two but Barby and I usually sipped weak shandies, not particularly enjoying them. It seemed it was the price to pay to be among our friends.

Before long, Peter and I moved to being officially 'together' and not enjoying being apart and as autumn approached he began to come over regularly at weekends either by bus or borrowing his Mum's car. He got on really well with my parents; they really liked him and were happy that I seemed to have found a soul mate. Like most of our generation then, we may not have been what was called 'intimate' in the bedroom department even when we became a 'couple' but as I have already tried to explain, we were intimate in a way that felt good and special such as sharing how we felt about life, ourselves, each other, other people, the future and our feelings. We held hands, gazed into each other's eyes, kissed, held each other close – what more can I say? It was a different world and although we knew sex wasn't only for having babies, (no, we weren't that naïve) all I can say is that yes, we may have been frustrated and yearning at times but we were, I suppose, programmed to wait for it, 'it' being sex within love and marriage and we never, ever thought of marriage as 'just a piece of paper'. Obviously, it wasn't easy and yes, of course there were those who didn't wait, they have their own stories and I'm not judging them or the way things are now, I'm only relating what I knew to be a widespread belief and attitude to relationships at that time of my life and while I understand how attitudes and many things have now changed and in some ways for the better, I do feel sad though in a way that what is now called 'having sex' used to be generally called 'making love'.

Well, enough of all that. On the Saturdays when Peter had a rugby match he would come over afterwards, arriving late and having to go back on the Sunday for work on Monday morning so it would be a very short visit. After one weekend like that, he phoned and said he didn't get the feeling that I appreciated the effort he made for us to have such a short time together and he was thinking of giving it a miss the next weekend. It was a shock! I felt terrible and it made me think that maybe he was right and I had been taking him and his regular visits for granted and I knew that to do that with someone you care about, or with anyone, is a 'no-no'. It was a 'wake up' call for me and I did what I could to reassure him and said I would understand if he only came over on 'no rugby' days. Anyway, Peter said it was time I went over there and met his family so it was agreed that I go over to Ilkley the following weekend, which although that sort of took the sting out of it, I really liked and felt good that he had been honest and straight with me about how he felt and that he gave me the chance to make amends.

Peter's Mum and Dad had divorced when he was 12 years old, a very rare and difficult thing to do back then and Peter told me it had affected him a lot and he had made a vow to himself that if and when he married, it would be forever.

I went on the train on Friday. I knew no-one could meet me so I got a cab to their house. Peter's Mum had recently re-married Hugh, who having served in the forces was now Principal of Keighley Art College, and, like Peter, would be still at work; so I had to introduce myself to the three women waiting to welcome me. And so, there was his Mum, who hugged me and said 'call me Kay', his Aunt, called Bunty and then there was Gaggy, his Grandmother, the matriarch of the family. Peter had told me about them all and how they all lived in the same house so I soon felt quite at ease even though I was anxious for Peter to arrive.

After leaving school early, like my brother had had to do, he had started a course in Engineering at night school, then went to Loughborough University where he had graduated in Production Engineering. As I've already told you he now worked in his Father's family firm of Gas Engineers in Keighley. His Father, also an Engineer, had remarried but lived and worked in Bristol. Peter had one sister, Jean, two years older who had recently married a farmer and lived near Carlisle. There was just the two of them so that was his immediate family. Bunty, I learned, had been briefly married to an American but had also been divorced and had no children.

Peter and Hugh arrived together as both travelled to and from Keighley by train each day, so there were a lot of hugs and hello's followed by much noisy activity in the kitchen preparing the evening meal before we all sat down to eat. Afterwards we helped with the clearing up and then Peter and I walked into Ilkley and spent a couple of hours in the Pub, talking mostly about the problem of our living so far apart, wanting to be together but not being able to afford it and what we could do about it. Peter worked very hard for his £5 a week; he said he would ask for a raise but knew it was unlikely he'd get it. Part of his job was erecting gas turbines which was a reserved occupation and had prevented him joining the forces, which he had tried to do although, being only a year older than me, it would have been at the tail end of things.

I wasn't much help either, as whatever I was doing in the hotel didn't warrant a wage. I was after all being housed and fed and wanted for nothing I needed. Peter gave his Mum £2 a week for his 'keep'. Most young people stayed at home until they married or moved away for some other reason such as a good job in another town. The usual thing was to save up to get married first and then gradually collect furniture and other things as you could afford them. Young married couples often stayed with parents until they had saved up enough to be able to rent somewhere or obtain a mortgage.

I enjoyed the weekend and getting to know Peter's family. They were an easy-going bunch, except perhaps for 'Gaggy' who was strictly of the 'old school' and seemed very concerned about my hair which she said was 'all over the place'. Well, I suppose she thought that a girl's hair ought to be pinned up and tidy and mine definitely wasn't. Peter assured me that she was 'like that' about a lot of things and not to take any notice and that he loved my hair and he loved my sloe eyes and he loved me! Well, whatever sloe eyes were, I didn't care! Those three little all important words 'I love you' were enough! This was different, real, honest, caring true! I stayed until Monday and left to catch the train after Peter had gone to work. I might as well have floated home on a cloud.

The AmDrams had chosen the autumn play which was to be *Rebecca* by Daphne du Maurier and I decided to ask Mums if I could read for the part of Mrs de Winter. Well, if you don't know the story, it's one of the two main characters. Soon after the hotel closed down in early October the play would be cast and rehearsals in the hotel dining room would get underway. No-one else read for the part of Mrs de W., so Mums said I could do it as long as I would learn my lines and take her direction, however tough and/or critical. I assured her I would and was really looking forward to the whole experience. Our new friend Gordon who had performed so well in *Flare Path* was once again persuaded, rather reluctantly, to take on the other lead part of Maxim de Winter.

Apart from school plays at Hildathorpe, this was my first 'go' at acting and I had a lot to learn. I knew everyone else in the cast, family friends or people I saw around town. Auntie Doff had the part of the unpleasant housekeeper who was so unkind to Mrs de Winter. Gordon and I used to get together outside of rehearsals and practice the scenes we had together, usually at his flat, Bobbie, his wife acting as our prompter and critic and I can tell you we mostly did more laughing than acting. Daddy would often hear me my lines and Peter could be persuaded to sometimes, if he was over at the weekend. The play sort of took over my life until finally it was for real and dress rehearsal day arrived and I was on the stage of the Spa

Theatre praying I wouldn't make a complete fool of myself, fall flat on my face, or forget my lines.

There was a buzz back stage, everyone wishing each other good luck or 'break a leg' which is what the pros say. Jimmy was as usual doing make-up and Hugh's set was brilliant and Win was reassuringly at her prompting position just off stage. Mums, (sorry) our producer, seemed to be very calm and having a final word with everyone before disappearing to view 'out front', no doubt with fingers firmly crossed that all would go well.

Well, it did go well, as did the following four performances and it was well attended and reviewed. I did become aware however that if I ever ventured to do any more stage work my voice was far too light and I would need to learn to project it. Anyway it had been a good experience and lots of fun and Peter came over for the Saturday night final show teasing me rotten about being a 'drama queen' but he said he was proud of me and I was so glad he was there. It was a bit of an anti-climax for a while afterwards but Bets and Eric's wedding was in December and shortly before that, in early November Princess Elizabeth was to be married to Prince Philip of Greece, which would be a really special and wonderful spectacle in London after all the drabness and desolation of the war years.

Aunt Sally made lovely red bridesmaid dresses for Midge and me and our bouquets were of red and white carnations. Being near to Christmas it seemed to fit, especially as there was a heavy snowfall the night before the wedding. Harry was Eric's Best Man and my brother Peter was a groomsman. There were about 150 guests and the reception was at James' Ballroom. It was another happy occasion.

Peter spent Christmas with us although he only had the two days, Christmas Day and Boxing Day off from work, so he couldn't go to the Golf Dance with me; but he did borrow his

Mum's car and drove over for New Year's Eve and the 'First Footing' and we both vowed to each other at midnight that by next year's end we would be nearer to being together, even though at that point we had no idea how.

Chapter 19

Be Happy, Ubs

THE SPRING PLAY was to be *Miranda* about a mermaid and Mums cast Midge in the main part. Midge told me that seeing me in *Rebecca* had encouraged her to 'have a go' which made up for the fact that I was a bit jealous, as I really fancied playing Miranda myself but as they say, 'that's Show Biz' and after all, I'd had my turn. Bets had a small part in it as well and Eric became involved and interested in the production side of things.

Bets and Eric had started their married life in a flat in Church Square on the same side and only a few yards from where we had lived before building the hotel. Many of the larger houses were being gradually turned into two or even three flats, which was much more practical and affordable as the cost of everything began to rise in response to Union demands and sometimes strikes for higher wages and better working conditions.

Peter had reluctantly given up playing rugby as he had twice been injured quite badly and not only had not been able to come over for the weekend, but also had to take time off from work which he couldn't afford to do.

Easter came and the hotel was open once more but bookings were down and with a full staff and the usual expenses it was more and more worrying for Daddy. We invested in some new advertising but the overseas holidays in the sun were gaining more and more customers and Whitby seemed to be attracting those who came only for a day out, often by coach many of which would park in the empty piece of land next to the Princess Royal and the occupants make straight for the beach or town centre shops and cafés then head home at the end of the day, not really any good for our mainly residential business.

Peter had asked his employers, who were also his Uncles for a raise in his wages, pleading that he was saving up to get married, but believe it or not they refused and he began to think of other ways he could improve the financial situation. He said with all those returning to full time jobs after war service plus most firms having guaranteed 'jobs for life' he saw little hope of moving to another Engineering Company even though he was prepared to go anywhere in the country. We talked about him applying to go in the Army, then at least we would be provided with somewhere to live but at some point we went off that idea, I can't remember why.

Daddy definitely wasn't his usual cheery self and seemed even more disoriented at times. He always dismissed any anxious queries Mums or I had, but as the season seemed to drag along we became more concerned about him. I would sometimes catch him in the office, leaning on his desk with his head in his hands but he wouldn't or perhaps couldn't say what was wrong apart from what we knew to be the worrying financial situation.

August proved to be good for business, and the hotel was fully booked for most of the month. Then as the weather remained fine well into September, there were quite a few casual bookings until season's end which perked things up quite a lot. Closing up time arrived and although Mums and Daddy moved straight away down to their first floor bedroom, I decided to stay in my top floor room until the weather turned colder. One morning I arrived downstairs to find the ambulance outside and Daddy on a stretcher being taken off to hospital. Mums told me he had been in a lot of pain overnight and she thought it was his heart. I felt so useless and worried – this was so much worse than anything else that had happened to us. Mums and I went separately to see him and when I went and sat beside his bed, he took hold of my hand and said, 'You will be happy, Ubs, won't you?' and I so wanted to say, 'You too Daddy' – but for some reason couldn't get the words out.

Late that night there was a phone call from the hospital telling us that Daddy's condition was worse and we 'should' go there. Mums and I sat in his room having to hear his laboured difficult breathing and not being able to do anything, while two nurses were either side of his bed but not seeming to do anything either. I remember just praying and praying that Daddy would get well but miserably sensing that he wasn't going to. Then our doctor appeared and insisted quite angrily that we go to the waiting room. I think Mums and I were in too much of a confused state to argue but thinking about it now it was a strange way to deal with such a situation and I think would be handled very differently now. After a while, the doctor came and told us that Daddy had died. He was just 54 years old. Mums and I went in and kissed him 'goodbye' then we walked home. I felt like dying too – it was the worst day of my life.

I didn't sleep for what was left of the night and I don't think Mums did either. The next day we had to phone my brother, our relatives in London and my Peter who came straight over to be with me. Then it was having to make arrangements for a funeral. Mums was really distraught and probably in a certain amount of shock which I think I was too so I don't know whether it helped me or not, but I began to take over making the arrangements. I remember one thing I especially tried to do was to have Daddy buried in a country village churchyard as I knew he would have liked that. Well, I soon found that it wasn't possible as you have to be resident or own a property in a place before you can be buried there, so we had to settle for a double plot in Whitby Churchyard which, in the end we decided to feel alright about. My brother too was devastated. Although he hadn't spent as much time with Daddy as I had, he had loved and appreciated him just as much and the unexpected shock of losing him so soon after returning from overseas really affected him. He and I did our best to comfort and support our Mums but we couldn't bring Daddy back.

The weeks after Daddy's funeral passed in a bit of a daze. I moved down to a first floor bedroom to be near Mums and her friends rallied round encouraging and supporting her to carry on with the next AmDram production; also, there was some sorting out to be done business-wise. Mums decided to put the hotel up for sale and (young) Eric who had trained as an Engineer but wanted to remain in Whitby offered to support me in the office during the following season until there was a sale. 'Jo' was sold and I was heartbroken – it was like Daddy leaving us all over again.

Peter was coming over regularly at weekends. I don't really know how I would have managed without him and his understanding of how I was feeling; also, he had applied for another job which was in Newcastle and meant he would be getting more money and that the job provided a car, if he got it that is. He said he wanted me to go over to Ilkley the following weekend so I asked Mums if she would be okay without me there and of course she said she would be. Before my brother went back to Reading Mums had talked to us together and said we were both to feel free to do whatever we chose and if it meant being away from her that she would be alright and we were not to worry about her. That was typical of my Mums but I assured her I wouldn't be going anywhere for some time – well, that was before my weekend in Ilkley.

I arrived quite late on the Friday so Peter was already there. He was looking quite pleased with himself and not surprising really when he told me he had got the Newcastle job and would start after Christmas. So, it was finally two fingers up to the family firm where he said he had 'worked his guts out' and they wouldn't even give him a measly £2 raise.

Later, when we were alone in the kitchen, guess what, he pulled me close to him and said, 'I think it's about time you had this' – and pulled out of his pocket a little box which when I opened it I saw the most beautiful object in the whole wide world inside winking at me: a platinum ring with two diamonds and no, he didn't actually say 'will you marry me' because we both already knew that's what we were aiming for, had been planning for and now just possibly might be able to do. Goodness knows how he had managed to save enough money for a diamond ring, well, any ring really, but I didn't ask. I was ecstatic and I made sure he knew I was. Peter's family already knew why he wanted me there for the weekend, and they all seemed very pleased for us and Hugh opened a bottle of bubbly. Later when I went to bed I sent a message to Daddy (via God): 'Don't worry Daddy, I'm happy.'

Chapter 20

Engagement, a Sort of Apprenticeship

BACK HOME AGAIN Mums said she was happy for me and asked if I was happy. I assured her that I was but felt sure she must be having mixed feelings when her life had been so recently thrown into turmoil and with important decisions to make about her own future. She was only 46 years old and although blessed with good health, energy and common sense, she had no experience of dealing with finance or balancing a budget. Daddy had always seen to that, and brother Peter and I were in no way qualified to give her advice, even if she had allowed us to which I doubt very much she would have.

Towards the end of the season, Bert and Nan, my London aunt and uncle, had put forward the idea, to Mums, Daddy and their friends that they organise a holiday in January to a Swiss ski resort, and the plans were being made at the time that Daddy died, although if he had lived I don't think, with his bad leg, he would have enjoyed it or even if he would have agreed to go. Anyway, Mums wasn't keen to go on her own even though Auntie Doff was going. In the end the others persuaded her to go and to take me along in Daddy's place as evidently it had all been paid for. It sounded wonderful as I'd never been on an actual holiday of any kind, unless you count the weekend in London. Daddy always said 'when you live in Whitby, you're on holiday all the time!' but, well, having just got engaged to Peter I wasn't happy to be going without him and I'm not sure that he was all that happy about me going without him either though he didn't actually say so.

Eventually I got used to the idea of the skiing holiday especially when I discovered young Eric and Bets were going; at least I wouldn't be the only young one among all the aunts and uncles and I did think it would be good for Mums as she certainly deserved a break and the mountain air would be a tonic for us all.

Peter came for Christmas and stayed for the whole week as he had finished working at Keighley and would start his new job in the New Year; brother Peter came too for a few days and brought his new girlfriend to meet us – she was called Betty and we all did our best to enjoy being together and to cope with Daddy not being there.

I'm sure Peter knew he could trust me – we trusted each other. We had become aware that we felt the same about most things and would support each other through thick and thin and it was a wonderful feeling. I knew he came from tough West Riding industrial stock and was ambitious to succeed in his profession and I made sure he knew I would support him in that, whatever it took. I had told Peter about Mac and how I had felt at the time but that I now knew that with us it was different, more mature and deeper, I had moved on. He said he couldn't respect Mac for not being honest about his marriage and was angry that I had been so hurt, also that he had had a few brief romances but none that had lasted very long. Basically we cleared the air on our previous love lives, such as they were and promised always to be honest with each other.

Mums bought some new ski pants and managed to borrow some from a friend for me and we got new padded jackets. Our skiing destination was Engelberg in Switzerland and involved much travelling, first to Basle where we boarded a little mountain train and climbed higher and higher through wonderful mountain scenery until we were finally in fairy land (well that's what it seemed like to me). We stayed in quite a large hotel and each morning were woken by a waiter who walked straight into our room with hot rolls and coffee. After getting kitted out with skis and ski boots we had to walk quite a long way to the 'nursery slopes' where hopefully we would learn how to ski'. After a few days when we had more or less managed to stay upright and mastered the 'snow plough' movement so we could stop, we all ventured higher up the mountain on the ski lifts with the intention of skiing down. Well, speaking only about my own effort, I managed to somehow get down the 'piste' mostly on my bottom. I didn't see much of the others, but I don't think they were much better than me. The next day I opted for a skating lesson on the rink opposite the hotel and went there for the rest of our stay. It seemed safer somehow.

We really enjoyed the food in the hotel, a lot of which was new to us, especially after the limited rations during the war. Win and Reg, being bakers, used to joke about it, especially the gorgeous puddings when they would say 'oh it's only a bit of praline' or some other dismissive remark and we would all tease them and say 'you're only jealous'!

In the evenings we all gathered in a small night spot called Matters where there was a small band and dancing and if you stayed late enough they served bacon and eggs. One day we walked along the main street with boutiques, jewellery and other shops filled with glamorous tempting things, most of which we hadn't seen since before the war or could afford – still, it was nice to see it all. Switzerland, after all, had been a neutral country during the war and had more or less carried on as normal.

Our magic week was soon over and apart from my poor skiing efforts I had enjoyed it and I think Mums, well everybody had too. I couldn't wait to tell Peter all about it and hope that we could have a similar holiday together one day.

Soon after we returned it was almost time to start the opening-up routine for the hotel and Mums was also quickly involved in production for the WADS spring play. I was in the office every day to deal with the post, enquiries or bills, etc. I suppose it was good that I had had time with Daddy to learn about it all, but I missed him so much and was anxious to get things right.

Mums and I had talked a bit about the wedding arrangements while we were away and decided to set the date for mid to late October when the hotel would be closed but we could manage to keep one or two of the staff on to help with things. Of course we asked Peter if he was okay with that and he said he was. We realised how we needed to make decisions then, as once the hotel was open and running it would be more difficult. I had lost no time in asking Barby and Bets to be my main two bridesmaids and Bobbie and Gordon's little girl, Susan, to be one too.

I decided to design my own wedding dress – well, make a sketch of how I would like it to be; perhaps it was partly to feel that my year at Art School wasn't a complete waste, not sure. Anyway, I made some sketches and Mums and I went over to Scarborough to see the Seamstress at one of the main Department Stores there and to choose the material. It was all very exciting. I could hardly believe it was happening. Anyway, after a lot of 'umming and ahrring' I decide on a cream Duchesse Satin for my dress with a replica of it for little Susan. We also chose turquoise blue lace for my two grown up bridesmaids. I had asked dear Aunt Sally if she would make the dresses for Barby and Bets and she said she would.

I think at that stage I was in a bit of a twilight zone or something because I wasn't giving a thought to what all this was going to cost. Mums, who would be paying for it all didn't mention money either; she seemed to be giving me free rein, carte blanche or whatever you like to call it, to have whatever I wanted and I don't remember questioning her about it but if I did I'm pretty sure she would have said that she just wanted me to have a nice wedding – for we both knew that is what Daddy would have wanted. I didn't want to think about that, about him not being there to 'give me away' although of course I would still have been 'his Ubs', wouldn't I?

I know I didn't at any point have doubts or second thoughts about marrying Peter. I think I asked him a couple of times if he did and he said 'no, of course not'. We were facing the world and our future together and no-one was going to stop us, at least that's what it felt like. He was working in Newcastle now and came over almost every weekend in his company car and I made sure he relaxed and had a pleasant time, often with a game of golf or a swim in the sea.

The hotel managed to open and one early guest was an elderly man who after a week decided to stay with us for the whole of the summer. One evening Peter and I 'bumped into' him at the Spa which was open again and we chatted with him for a while telling him of our plans and he told us he had recently been widowed and missed his wife very much. After that, when I would see him around or when I was in the reception/office, we would have a chat and if he could catch sight of Peter at the weekends he would talk for a while to him also. His name was Alfred.

As time went on we became aware that Alfred seemed to be starting to depend on meeting up with us and although we liked him and knew he was rather lonely, we had to start sometimes trying to avoid him which felt a bit unkind but he was sort of taking us for granted. Imagine our surprise when one weekend he cornered Peter and said he wanted to 'adopt' us and that he had plenty of money and could help us out, pay for our honeymoon, etc. Well, as you know we had little or no savings to start our married life and would be living on Peter's salary, so don't think we didn't consider Alfred's offer – but not for long: we both agreed it just didn't seem right. We hardly knew the dear man and we both felt we wanted to take care of ourselves and not be indebted in some way, so rightly or wrongly we declined Alfred's generous offer.

Anyway Peter was earning more now and saving like mad and don't forget I had my Yorkshire Penny Bank savings which must have grown to all of £100, even though my Saturday payments had stopped when I joined the WRNS. Peter had started looking around Newcastle for somewhere for us to live and it seemed like to rent a flat was going to cost between £3 and £4 a week.

I was managing in the office okay and Eric came over to help me with the accounts once a week as he had promised. We were really too busy to think about whether there was any interest in buying the hotel or how Mums was going to manage if it didn't sell and I had moved to Newcastle. We were very busy in August and it was difficult to find time to think about the wedding. We had managed to send out the invitations and of course the reception was to be at our friends Reg and Win's place, James' Ballroom, and their gift to us was to be the Wedding Cake which was very kind.

Somehow Mums and I together with Bobbie and little Susan managed to get over to Scarborough for fittings. Bobbie said she felt a bit envious as she and Gordon had married in their uniforms at a register office. I tried not to feel guilty but part of me did – I really wasn't sure I deserved what was happening to me.

Chapter 21

Happy and Hopeful

SEPTEMBER CAME and the weather stayed warm and sunny so we were still quite busy. One day we had a surprise visit from Peter's Grandma, Gaggy and his Aunty Bunty who had lunch and then, as we were chatting in our little private room, Gaggy started to take off her blouse saying it was far too hot and proceeded to sip her coffee quite happily in her bra and vest. Bunty didn't turn a hair so we didn't either, I mean what was wrong, she was hot and I suppose old so why not? But we did have a laugh afterwards and when Peter arrived at the weekend he said, 'Oh, that's my Grandma, quite normal!'

Gaggy had told me that her wedding gift to us was to be a bedroom suite and I was to choose one and send her the bill. I was so touched and excited. Mums had said she would pay for all the carpets once we had found a flat and also give us any furniture from the hotel that we needed. Other gifts were beginning to arrive such as a set of towels from Holly and Basil and I couldn't wait for the Hotel to close and concentrate on it all.

At last on October 4th we finally closed the hotel, but instead of the complete end-of-season routine it was a re-organising and preparation for family/relatives coming to stay. The wedding was to be on the 17th which was also the day my parents had been married, so we had just over two weeks to do what still had to be done. Peter and I went to see the minister who would take the service and to be honest I wasn't very impressed with him; he didn't say anything to us that was very helpful and Peter agreed with me – you would think we were asking him not to marry us as his manner seemed almost disapproving. Maybe we weren't regular church goers but we loved each other and believed in a loving power for good which we called God and the fact that we chose to be married in church surely proved that; well, we had to accept this grumpy guy would make us married so that was that.

Even though St Hilda's church was only round the corner from the hotel, we still needed to order wedding cars, didn't we – flowers, the choir, etc.? Somehow it all got done and before we knew it, it was the day before. My beautiful dress had arrived and was hanging up in what we thought of as the best bedroom which Mums had let me have for the day. Our London relatives had arrived to stay with us, also Barby and my brother who was to 'walk me down the aisle' – well, give me away, so to speak. Peter's best man, Leslie, an old friend and his girlfriend were staying somewhere else but came to visit with us in the evening. We had a fire in the main lounge and dear Louie helped Mums to cook an evening meal for everyone.

Peter was to spend the night with our friends Eric and Madge. I think he and Leslie and my brother went out for a pint or two but that was what his Stag Night amounted to and although Hen Nights didn't happen then, I enjoyed the gathering we had with me being the centre of attention. That night I went to bed in the hotel's very best room gazing happily at my cream duchesse satin dress, the cream satin shoes and the cream tulle veil and sent a little prayer to my Daddy (via God): 'I am very happy but I do so wish you were here.'

The wedding was at 2 p.m. so there was all morning to get ourselves ready. I have to confess that when I woke up I had to make a dash for the loo! I suppose I was nervous, maybe even worried. Breakfast was a 'help yourself' but I couldn't eat a thing. I think I had a cup of tea and kept my bathrobe on all morning until it was time to get into the bridal gear.

Well, a hug from Mums before she went off alone and then it was time for my brother Peter and I to pile into the waiting car to drive the few yards to the church. The photographer was waiting along with a few onlookers and just as we made our way to the entrance I realised I had left my bouquet back at the hotel. Peter said 'don't worry' and set off to sprint back the short distance to get it. A slight delay, but it made me traditionally (though only a few minutes) late!

After that, everything went off as planned. Most importantly Peter, my Mr Very Right and I were married. We had hardly any money but we had each other, our dreams and ambitions and most important of all, we had love which is really all you need.

Isn't it?

My Father Said

My Father said
Never go away
Without the means to pay
For your return

And use your head
Before you sit
On a rain-soaked
Bit of grass

He didn't need to say
he cared
Love was in his eyes
And his reluctance to goodbyes

With wisely word or knowing look
Gentle smile, quick to forgive
The quiet way he met each day
And so much still to give

He died

But I never go away
Without the means to pay
For my return

And never, never sit on wet grass

EDC

Printed in Poland
by Amazon Fulfillment
Poland Sp. z o.o., Wrocław